Confessions of a Church Felon

Protecting Your Ministry from the Flames of Fraud

Glenn A. Miller
Jeffrey A. Klick
Rodney A. Harrison

What Others Are Saying

"One of the quickest ways to shipwreck your ministry and tarnish your integrity is to have financial indiscretions. Fraud not only causes personal pain and heartache, but the fallout and collateral damage impacts a myriad of others and causes great harm to the body of Christ. The fact that fraud is so prevalent should motivate us to utilize every means necessary to safeguard our ministries. *Confessions of a Church Felon* is a great resource for leaders who want to fireproof their ministries. The authors bring together a wealth of knowledge and experience to provide a practical resource for Christian ministries."

Anthony W. Allen
President Hannibal-LaGrange University

Rodney Harrison, Jeffrey Klick, and Glenn Miller have just written in *Confession of a Church Felon: Protecting your Ministry from the Flames of Fraud*, the quintessential work on church fraud and what churches, lay leaders, and pastors can do about it! Do not miss Chapter Four on the *Fraud Triangle* because that is conceivably the most important chapter in the entire book. This is a book about Church Administration but it is more than the usual work listing procedures and policies. It is a sobering look at what happens when churches do not develop the safety nets for keeping ones church secure. Buy this book for everyone on your staff and all of your lay leaders who work in the arena of finances and administration. You will not regret it!

Tom Cheyney
Founder & Directional Leader
Renovate National Church Revitalization Conference

Confessions of a Church Felon is a clarion call for the church to embrace accountability and seek integrity in its finances. By unpacking real-life examples of church fraud, *Confessions of a Church Felon* examines the potential risk of financial fraud and abuse that all churches face. This book provides easy to understand, yet powerful tools that every church should implement to reduce this risk. Starting with a discussion on why fraud occurs, to documenting specific controls needed to protect church finances, to providing wise pastoral guidance on what to do if a church experiences fraud, the authors share their vast experience and knowledge to help leaders navigate this journey. Their love for the local church shines through as they provide strategies and best practices to improve financial integrity in the church. Whether you've experienced fraud in the past, or just want to strengthen and protect your ministry moving forward, this book will provide the tools necessary to "fireproof" your ministry. As someone who has helped churches recover from the devastating consequences of fraud, I can attest that this book isn't just for the bookkeeper in your church, but should be required reading for every ministry leader!

Rollie Dimos, CIA, CFE, CISA
Internal Audit Director,
The General Council of the Assemblies of God

As a Church Consultant I dread three phone calls. The first comes from a small group of concerned members who want to "fire their Pastor". The second phone call comes from a member of a church where the Pastor has sold off church properties and facilities and pocketed the money for himself directly or through a dummy nonprofit organization he owns and directs. The third phone call comes from a member of a church finance committee who has discovered that their Pastor, a staff member, or an elected officer in the church has been stealing money from the church. All three scenarios lead to years of turmoil and church conflict. In the case of direct stealing in the church by trusted leaders we end up asking the church a number of key questions?

- Why were no safe guards put in place over the years?
- Who is accountable for reviewing the spending of the Pastor, Staff, and elected officers who handle the church's money?
- Who oversees the counting and depositing of the weekly offerings?
- Does the church have a sound and reasonable set of financial policies and procedures?

In a perfect church world this book would be totally unnecessary. Pastors and officers would live out their Christian faith with integrity and honesty. Based on the casual approach most churches take regarding their finances it is a surprise that the thievery discussed by the Pastor of the church across the street doesn't happen more often. (Maybe it does!)

Confessions of a Church Felon targets a very special new problem facing today's casual approach to church life. The book will be useful for local church leadership groups who are assigned the task of overseeing church finances. It will also serve as an excellent seminary textbook and Continuing Educational tool for current church leaders.

Dr. Randy L. Bennett
President, California Southern Baptist Convention
Director of Missions, Kern County Southern Baptist Association

Jesus loves His bride, the church. Someday the church will be "without spot or wrinkle"... "holy and without blemish" (Ephesians 5:27). Until that day, the church must be diligent to display the supreme beauty and integrity of Christ to a lost and dying world. This book is a helpful and practical guide for church leaders who want manage their church finances with confidence and integrity.

Lincoln VerMeer
Vice President, Church Banking Team
Cass Commercial Bank

A great book that gives solid, concrete advice and explanations about fraud, where it comes from, how to avoid it, and how to deal with it when it occurs. I think it's also important to point out that it is written by authors who have extensive experience in church leadership, pastoring, administration, accounting and finance, as well as skill and knowledge in preventing and addressing fraud in churches and schools. It's also a "must have" for pastors, seminary grads, church board members, treasurers and anyone else who deals with accounting/finance in churches and schools. Furthermore, the book's guidance is helpful for any size organization, whether you're a small rural church, a mid-sized seminary or a large multi-campus church.

Ken Mestemacher
Business Administrator
Lenexa Baptist Church

"My firm has served churches for over thirty years. Sadly, we have seen the incidents of financial fraud increase to near epidemic levels over those years, diverting precious resources, disrupting church operations, harming church personnel and tarnishing the reputation of churches in general. This book provides a much needed, basic resource for church boards and management to help protect their church "from the flames of fraud."

John A. Parrish, MBA, CPA, CFE
Partner, Keller & Owens, LLC

As a church insurance specialist for almost 35 years, I wholeheartedly recommend this book to every church leader desiring financial integrity in their ministry. The stories and resulting damage to the Kingdom are far too familiar. My father, a pastor for over 50 years, frequently cautioned, "It is better to prepare and prevent than need to repair and repent." These authors offer practical tools to effectively safeguard your ministry.

Becky Moyer
Moyer & Moyer Insurance Agency, Inc.

Dedications

To my wife Kim, who has faithfully supported me these last 36 years allowing me to follow my dreams. – Glenn

To all the pastors who labor for the Kingdom wondering if their labors matter - they do, and someday you will hear, "Well done good and faithful servant" from our Lord Jesus. – Jeff

To the church, the Bride of Christ, and the leaders who wisely protect her from the Evil One's schemes. – Rod

Special Thanks

We would like to acknowledge and thank Chris Miller for his work on the cover design and help with all the special formatting needed with those helpful forms in the appendix. We also grateful for Kim Farmer and her sharp eye tirelessly hunting for all those commas and such – Thank you both!

Contents

Introduction

I am a Christian.
I am a church administrator.
I am a thief. ~Sam

Giving is down, people are quitting, and the overall interest in the Church, the Bride of Christ, is trending down hill. Trust has been broken, lives have been damaged, and reputations destroyed. In short, the last few decades for the glorious Church have been challenging.

One dimension of this decline is the lack of knowledge and understanding by Her leaders. Jesus said He would build His Church and He will not fail, however, His under-shepherds are making the task difficult at times!

1

I (Glenn) was speaking at a church conference in Orlando when I received an urgent text from one of my staff, "Call me immediately, we have a problem." That was an unusual text given that we have well trained staff, good managers, and we seldom encounter a situation that would merit that kind of text. So I called her and asked what the problem was. She said she and her administrative audit team were in route to a new church client when she got a call from the church informing her that the father of the Senior Pastor had just resigned as bookkeeper and admitted to stealing from the church for several years. I had met with this very church one year before and shared with them that their systems and staffing left them vulnerable, but no action was taken, clearly a lack of knowledge and a lack of understanding.

Most of us do not have to think long before the names and faces of leaders who have failed enter our recollection. Some, very well known nationally, have done unthinkable damage to themselves, their families, and to their churches. Immorality and financial fraud continues to take its toll on the Body of Christ. This must change and it can change beginning today!

This passion for change is why we are writing this book. The Church of Jesus Christ has suffered through enough failed leaders' sinful behavior. We must increase our knowledge and understanding if we are to help prevent these kinds of ministry ending events. We cannot claim that what we are sharing with you will prevent *all* failure in the ministry, but we do promise that if you read and *implement* what we share, we can reduce it significantly! Sinful humans will always find a way to express their sin, but we should not make it easy for them to do so!

Our first effort as a team of writers was entitled *Pastoral Helmsmanship: A Pastors Guide to Church Administration*. This book has rapidly become a textbook and handbook for seminaries and pastors across the nation. Why? Because pastors are woefully undertrained in the realities of real pastoral duties faced once the student leaves the classroom.

Even as we finished the last details and thoughts on our first book together, we all knew it would not be our last. There simply is too much yet to be done and too much at stake. Even in a book exceeding 380 pages, we simply could not cover everything that needed to be said regarding church administration.

As we consider the needs of the Church, we are both saddened and enthused to share this next work with you. We are deeply saddened that such a book is necessary, but pleased that we have the ability to help with this pressing need. Our desire is to help the Church by educating Her leaders to step up in all aspects of integrity. Quite simply, we want to "raise the standard" across the theological spectrum.

The title of this work is taken from an actual fraud case and a workshop we present through The Institute for Church Management. It is one of the most popular courses offered. Again, although sad on one hand, the popularity speaks to the necessity of the topics covered.

Most people would not intentionally want to live in a home nor attend a church that was labeled as a "Fire Hazard." While somewhat more acceptable, the term "Fire Resistant" is better, yet still not where most of us would like to dwell. What would bring comfort and assurance to us is the term "Fireproof," and that is what we are pursuing with this book – providing security from the devastation and destruction caused by fraud in ministry.

We will show how every church, regardless of their size or resources, can "up their game" in this important area and to increase integrity while decreasing the occurrence of fraud. Gaining knowledge and understanding and preventing fraud does not have to cost a lot of money and we will show you how to accomplish this task.

There is always some expense to improve quality and control over finances, but we all know you get what you pay for. Cutting corners and being sloppy with integrity costs the Church more than we can, or should be willing, to pay. Remember the feeling you had the last time the mainstream media had a good laugh at yet another high-profile Christian leader being led away in handcuffs, or living a life contrary to what they had boldly proclaimed? This does not have to happen in your church.

Glenn Miller is a Certified Fraud Examiner and has extensive experience dealing with large numbers of these types of cases. Rodney Harrison is a seminary professor and often serves as a transitional pastor who has helped multiple churches clean up after the previous pastor left the church in shambles by their sinful behavior. Jeff Klick has been an administrator and pastor for more than three decades and has helped many churches walk through the aftermath of financial and sexual failure. Sadly, the authors have acquired far too many firsthand experiences with these tragic events in the Church we all love.

That's the bad news. The good news is that God is a redeeming God. Jesus will build His Church and the gates of hell will not overcome Her! We believe that the experiences gained through dealing with these tragic occurrences can be utilized for the greater good.

A disclaimer of sorts is necessary before reading the rest of this book. Each tragic story shared in the following pages is, sadly, true. Names and circumstances have been modified to protect the innocent, but the essence of the real events has been preserved. The main storyline, one of the most in-depth and complex fraud cases we have encountered, took place at "The Church Across Town." We picked this name because many feel that this is "someone else's problem" or "this could never happen to us" type thinking. As you finish this book, we pray that this false thinking will change into a "this will not happen to us" mindset instead!

At the end of each chapter we will include actual testimony from the people who are the key players in this tragic, yet redemptive, event. The names we will use are: Pastor Bill, the senior pastor; Treasurer Cindy, the church treasurer; and Administrator Sam, the church administrator. Each of these has voluntarily given us their perspective for this book in recorded conversations. Their hope, like ours, is that God would use these painful remembrances to help other people who find themselves in similar circumstances. Even more importantly, we all pray that this sharing will help others to avoid going down the same destructive path. We greatly appreciate their sacrifice in recounting the events and their feelings so that we may all benefit. May God richly bless them for their efforts.

We pray as you read these pages that your heart would be stirred, your thought patterns challenged, and effectual change would be implemented. The world around us is waiting for the Church to present a difference and for our actions to align with our words. Let the difference begin with each of us.

While the book primarily focuses on financial fraud, many of the principles can be used to reduce sexual failure as well. The sin of immorality is just as fraudulent as financial theft is and the damaged caused to the Body of Christ is devastating.

There is hope for those trapped in sin and there is life after death for the church that goes through the devastation of moral or financial failure. We have included two chapters detailing how to walk through the process of dealing with these issues, and also how to not only survive, but to redeem them.

1 Real People, Real Pain, and a Real Problem

Well, it was sin that had taken over my thought process.
~ Sam

The pastor was a dynamic speaker and possessed excellent relational skills. His smile and winsomeness could calm an angry person in a matter of minutes. A natural leader, who could silence a room by simply walking in to it, never appeared to be ruffled. This leader, surrounded by people who loved and supported him, could do no wrong. Well, at least until he had stolen a large sum of money and taken his girlfriend (notice, not his wife) on an around-the-world trip.

The church was shaken. The leadership, paralyzed and stunned in disbelief, simply did not know what to do next. Eventually, the once large and impacting ministry folded and was soon absorbed by a large, growing church that wanted to expand in that part of the city. Many members left and never returned. Some walked away from their faith and others simply became a bit more cynical. The local papers rejoiced, the youth mocked, and the church's good name received a fatal wound.

How could this happen? Could it have been prevented? What was missing in this church for these crimes to take place? "Who knew what?" and "When did they know?" type questions still circulate today, years after the fact. What were the leaders doing? If they didn't know, why didn't they? "Someone has to pay for this" was a common theme. It is usually the leaders who remain to try to heal up the brokenhearted, and, unfortunately, who end up paying the heaviest price.

While there are answers to all of these questions, most of them will go unanswered. Several important questions we can answer are:

- How could this have been prevented?
- What systems should have been in place to guard against such behavior?
- Once suspected or detected, how should we have handled this?
- What can we do to help protect our church?

While we don't fully understand why someone chooses to walk away from a successful ministry by stealing or committing sexual immorality, we do have an understanding of the pain caused by his or her actions. Spouses, children, extended family members, fellow leaders, and those who followed these leaders are often left disillusioned. The wages of sin are always death, and when a leader lies, cheats, steals, and gives in to immorality, the damage to the Kingdom is significant.

I (Glenn) received a call from a pastor who wanted to hire our accounting firm to do his church's books. We met, went through the process, and they signed up to convert to our service. We emailed and called the treasurer over a several month period, but he never returned our correspondence. After a few months, the pastor called and asked for financial reports and I informed him that the treasurer had never gotten back with us to implement the conversion.

Upon further investigation, the church discovered that the treasurer had been diverting funds for several years to his favorite mission's agency. Tens of thousands of dollars had been redirected.

While the funds were given to an organization, when this fraudulent behavior was discovered, anger and lack of confidence in the leadership eventually led to the destruction of this church.

After several months of very messy and angry meetings, the church closed. A good ministry completely destroyed because of a lack of knowledge and understanding regarding financial accountability. Every time I drive by their empty building, I just shake my head and say "What a shame; this did not have to happen."

Nationally, research has spotlighted the incredible magnitude of the problem of fraud in churches and ministries:

> According to the Status of Global Mission report from the Center for the Study of Global Christianity, Christians worldwide committed more than $39 billion in church-related financial fraud during the first half of 2014. Compare that to the $35 billion churches spent on worldwide mission work during the same time frame.[1]

Church crime continues to grow—estimated at $110 million each day. Increasing at an annual rate of nearly six percent, researchers expect church financial fraud to reach the $60 billion mark by 2025. That's still not the whole picture. About 80 percent of all cases of church fraud go unreported, and therefore, are not included in statistics. Only the big fraud cases, some involving complex schemes perpetrated by well-known Christian individuals and organizations, make the news.

The numbers are so large they are hard to comprehend, and yet, as large as they are, we continue to, for the most part, ignore the problem. Can you imagine if we prevented even a small percentage of fraud, how those funds could be used? We are talking about billions of ministry dollars each year that could be spent on reaching the lost for Christ, feeding and clothing the homeless, drilling fresh water wells in Africa, planting new churches around the world, and other ministries only limited by our imaginations and lack of funds.

---

[1]http://www.brotherhoodmutual.com/index.cfm/resources/ministrysafety/article/church-fraud/

But church fraud seems so improbable. This type of sinful behavior would never happen in our church. We have good honest people here, right?

"The Church Across Town"

The church was decades old, well established, and located in suburbia, USA. With the retirement of the long-term church administrator, it was time to find a replacement. I (Glenn) was asked to do some interim church administration work and help them find a replacement. As time progressed, we found a very suitable person, a long- term member of the church, and we hired him. Sam was well respected by the congregation and things seemed to be off to a great start. The church treasurer, Cindy, being good friends with this church member, was very pleased to have him on board.

After the first year or so, as I was going through the bank statements, I noticed a check made out to Sam, the church administrator, only signed by Sam, the church administrator, made out for several thousand dollars. I was deeply concerned as to what this was, so I immediately alerted Senior Pastor Bill, and we took Administrator Sam to lunch. We confronted him about the large check written to himself and he remorsefully explained that he was just "borrowing" those funds temporarily because he got behind in his house payments. He said that the church had helped lots of people in the same situation from the benevolence fund, so he thought for certain that he would have been approved, but he didn't have time to go through the process. He, of course, intended to pay the money back.

Disappointed and a bit bewildered, Pastor Bill and I decided to believe him, and let him off with a stern warning, "This will never happen again!" It seemed redemptive and appropriate at the time.

In the coming months Administrator Sam began to change. He missed work, missed meetings, and missed reporting deadlines, and his work became further and further behind. When I asked him how he was doing, he made reference to some personal issues he was having outside of work and that he found it more and more difficult to concentrate on his church work. We prayed for him, and sent him back to work.

Little did we know at that time, what the next twelve months would bring. After more evidence of financial fraud was discovered, Pastor Bill explained:

Pastor Bill: My assistant one day had made the comment, "Are you okay?" because he had noticed that I was crying all the time. And I was sighing deeply on a regular basis. "You know," he said, "for weeks you've been crying all the time. Are you okay? Is something wrong?"

Real people...real pain...and a real problem.

Action Questions

1. Describe your feeling when you read some of these true stories. Are you angry, sad, depressed or _____? Why?

2. What counsel and comfort would you offer to a church or ministry that has just discovered fraud?

3. What would your first sermon be to the congregation the Sunday after the fraud became public knowledge? Why?

4. Would you like to not have to answer questions 1-3 regarding your ministry? Read on!

2 Illusions, Myths, and Excuses

...and I'm still having a hard time with this whole situation because of my sin. And I know you are supposed to confess and let it go, but it's one of those things... ~Sam

"Those stories in the previous chapters are tragic, but that simply would never happen at our church. Our pastor is great! Our leaders would never fall to temptation in that way. Our treasurer is the best person ever. He has been handling our church finances for over twenty years and we have never had a problem (that we know of). We have known these people for many, many years; they simply could never be guilty of stealing or fraud." Really?

If you reread the stories in the previous chapters, we assure you that none of the people involved were known criminals before volunteering or being hired. They were all professing Christians, one even a parent! A parent...can you imagine? None of them were associated with unsavory characters or closet underworld crime figures. Each of them were well known, dearly loved, and respected. Each were professing Christians, and yet, they ended up lying, stealing, and committing sinful acts that stole Kingdom resources, God's money, from the church! It is an illusion to think that those people were some special type of sinners and our people are not capable of such behaviors.

"In order to become disillusioned, one must first have an illusion" is one of the author's favorite sayings. It is an illusion to believe that anyone is beyond temptation and capable of sin. In fact, that belief is not a biblical one.

> Brothers, if anyone is caught in any transgression, you who are spiritual should restore him in a spirit of gentleness. Keep watch on yourself, lest you too be tempted.
>
> Galatians 6:1 (ESV)

> But each person is tempted when he is lured and enticed by his own desire. Then desire when it has conceived gives birth to sin, and sin when it is fully grown brings forth death.
>
> James 1:14-15 (ESV)

16

No person is beyond temptation, and only One lived a perfect life never giving into it. We will delve into this false understanding that "this could not happen in our ministry" more in the next chapter, but for now, the short answer is, "Yes it can."

Case in Point

It was a small country church with a faithful congregation of thirty people. These dear saints were the salt of the earth type people, ministering in any way they could to their small community. The leaders called and wanted to go on our accounting service (Miller Management Systems, LLC) and we were glad to help. The treasurer was assigned the task to meet with us and help with the conversion. (Sound familiar?)

After several months of dodging our communications, the senior pastor intervened and forced a meeting to convert the books over to our service. My staff came back to the office and began their work. Within two hours, they came to my office, and I could tell by the look on their faces it was bad news, and they said, "We have another one." I knew immediately "another one" meant another fraud case.

Upon inspection of the books, giving records, and bank statements, we immediately discovered that the treasurer had been stealing $60.00 every other week for years. The treasurer was counting the offering, taking a person's cash tithe, and adding the amount on their annual giving statement to avoid detection. It was "almost" undetectable.

The treasurer resigned in disgrace causing pain and heartache to many relationships. He went to another church and tried the same thing; the only problem was that we were already doing that church's books! God will not be mocked – sin will be uncovered and proclaimed. How much suffering could have been avoided if simple techniques were in place earlier?

There are many myths that circulate when you begin to dialog about the topic of fraud:

- It is an isolated experience; it would never happen to us.
- Only large churches and ministries need to be concerned.
- This is only a problem in the big city.
- The people involved must not have really been Christians.
- We trust everyone, therefore fraud won't happen here.
- It would cost way too much to implement fraud control measures.
- We have always done it this way and changing is too hard.
- If we change things now, we will offend some people.
- If we make any policy changes, people will think something bad just happened.
- It really does not matter that much; it is not that big of a deal.

There are others of course, but just glancing over this list should alert us to some real problems. A lack of knowledge and understanding on the part of pastors and lay leaders will not make the issue go away, nor will wishful thinking. Fraud is real, churches are being destroyed, and the truth is, most of it could be easily prevented!

Let's take these misconceptions one at a time and think about them a bit further.

It Is an Isolated Experience

Studies show that fraud is anything but isolated. As noted earlier, church fraud is on the rise and has now reached billions of dollars annually. The main reason why many people think it is so isolated is because of the approach most churches are using when fraud is discovered, which includes denial and refusal to deal with it.

One church hired us to investigate suspected fraud by a lay leader. We did the investigation and presented the evidence. As a Certified Fraud Examiner, we are not permitted to make accusations, only perform investigations and present findings. In this case, the evidence very clearly pointed to fraud. They said, "Thank you for your report." End of meeting. When I asked if they had questions, they said, "No." Do you need any additional help planning on how to handle this? "No. We are not going to deal with it. He is no longer a church member and if we bring up the findings now, he might sue us, and the congregation will most certainly be angry with leadership. It will only end up hurting the church. Thanks." For the record, I think it is best if I do NOT share my true feelings about their leadership at this time.

Another church hired us to look into a church administrator who they feared might be playing a bit fast and loose with his credit card. After we found a consistent pattern of misuse of funds via credit card, the pastor once again said, "Thanks, we're good." When I pressed him a bit, he responded, "He is no longer is on staff. It will just hurt the church, hurt the people, open us up to a potential law suite, and it will make leadership look stupid." (Too late.) Sorry, did I say or write that out loud? This fraudster went on his way and started a new church. What a disservice to the Kingdom!

Only Large Churches and Ministries Need to Be Concerned

Statistically, the size of the church has nothing to do with the instances of fraud. The issues involved are ease of access to funds, lack of controls, and accountability, not how many members there are in the pews. Since nearly 90% of US churches have less than 100 members, it would stand to reason that the smaller churches would have a larger percentage of fraud cases than the larger ones.

This is Only a Problem in the Big City

The size of the city does not matter, for sin knows no bounds or geographical regions. While it is true that the larger cities will have more people and churches, the ratio of Christians to non-Christians in those cities and churches really does not change. All it takes is one thief to ruin a church regardless of the size of the city it resides in.

It was the new pastor's first Sunday in a small town known for winning football teams, friendly people, and a hometown hero from American Idol. The previous pastor, despite a great track record of service, left the church in a financial free fall, with offerings falling $300-$500 below budget each week. During the offering, the pastor noticed that the money appeared to be given to one person, who left the auditorium to put the offering into the counting room. Knowing this practice left the church open to both fraud, or, at a minimum, suspicion, the pastor met with the ushers a week later, instructing them on best practices for money handling. Despite this meeting, the following week the offering process appeared unchanged. This story will be continued shortly.

The People Involved Were Not Christians

While it is true that some who commit fraud may not be Christians, it is hard to make that statement about all of them. We can report that 100% of the cases that Miller Management Systems, LLC has dealt with over the past ten years, the fraudsters were all professing Christians. Most of the people who end up lying, cheating, and stealing from the church were serving in important positions and were at one time influential leaders in the church. Only the Lord Jesus knows the real spiritual condition of someone, but not every pastor or treasurer we have encountered who stole money was unsaved. They simply chose to sin. We will let the Lord deal with the eternal ramifications of such choices; we will attempt to help deal with the earthly ones.

We Trust Everyone

"If all you look for is evil, you will find it," some have stated. "You want to establish all these controls, no wonder everyone starts thinking about stealing. Law produces the desire to steal," some believe. This is not a theological book, so we won't explore that trail; however, simply blindly trusting everyone is a sure way to encourage abuse. Do you lock your house at night or your car? Do you attempt to park under a light when you go shopping at night? Do you leave your wallet or purse laying around with money in it and never give it another thought? Do you look both ways before crossing a street? Don't you just trust everyone? Do you balance your bank statement? We trust, but verify. We also trust those in the church, but we want to help limit their temptations and potential failure. We want to trust and protect the individuals, and at the same time, protect the church.

Remember the new pastor in the small town recently mentioned? The pastor decided to look into the accounting process from collection to deposit. Two counters required; check. Two signatures required for checks and deposit slips; check. The accounting and deposit procedures were appropriate. However, was all of the cash reaching the counters? Cash contributions in small towns are still very common. For the next few Sundays, several uncommon denominations of cash ($2 and $50 bills) were placed in the offering. The receipt of these bills, however, was not reflected in the weekly counting sheet. Either someone was making "change" with the bills during the offering, or a trusted member was behaving badly.

It Costs Too Much to Implement Fraud Control

In the coming chapters we will show you many changes you can make that will cost your church (in dollars and cents) absolutely nothing. Zero. Nada. What it will cost is time and discipline to follow the established controls. There may also be the political cost of making changes in policies and procedures and possibly offending someone. The vast majority of anti-fraud controls are simply common sense items to be performed with very little financial costs. Yes, there are some things we are going to recommend that will cost a little money, but most of them will not.

Perhaps a re-evaluation of the word "cost" is in order. We tend to think in terms of dollars and cents where we should be thinking in terms of value and what is gained, or avoided. What is the true cost of a ministry being destroyed by fraud compared to implementing a few procedures to prevent it? Helping someone overcome a temptation to steal and ruin their lives, hurt their family and ruin the good name of your church is worth how much again?

Maybe if we thought of anti-fraud tools in terms of insurance it would make more sense. We purchase insurance on our car, house, and ourselves to provide financial protection against some future event that may or may not happen. We really don't appreciate the value of the money spent on insurance until it is needed. If you watch your house burn down, your auto being repaired after a crash, or the bills paid for after surgery, you gain a better perspective of the "cost" of insurance. The money spent was well worth it when the tragedy occurs.

Whatever we end up spending in time and money to prevent fraud is only fully appreciated and realized as we observe the pain, suffering, and reputations ruined by not spending the time and money in advance to prevent it. It does not cost too much to prevent fraud; it costs too much to not do so.

We Have Always Done It This Way and Changing Is Too Hard

Change *can* be hard, but failure to adapt, grow, and perform our duties with increasing integrity and care often leads to devastation. Replacing a long-term, faithful offering counter with a team *may* cause hard feelings, but finding out that the person has been stealing cash for years can cripple your ministry's reputation. Which one really is harder in the long term?

Return with us one more time to the new pastor in the small-town church. The process used for collecting and counting the offering was designed for the convenience of the volunteers. By taking the offering early in the service, the money counters could tally the offering during the service, and depart for Perkin's or home with the rest of the congregation. As expected, the recommended changes as to how and when the offering was taken were met with resistance by some. However, the pastor prevailed, and the changes were implemented, moving the offering to the end of the service. Once collected, at least two ushers took the money to the counting room. And the offerings, well, they magically increased by $500 per week.

Change is one of the few constants in life. The real question is not if we should change, but which direction should we be heading? Are we leading our ministries towards financial integrity, strong internal controls that will preserve our good name we worked so hard to achieve, or towards a fraud disaster? Implementing change may end up being the best decision ever made in this area.

We are not denying the reality of potentially hurt feelings and some push back from people who resist change; we are simply saying that there is too much at stake not to continue down the path of good policies and procedures that will protect your ministry.

If someone is overly resistant to the change that will ensure the protection and reputation of all involved in the area of finances, we have to explore the reasons why. After we explain the reasons behind the necessary changes being implemented, most people will adapt quickly. Unless there is something amiss, good internal controls and procedures offer protection to the ones involved and will be accepted.

If We Change Things Now, We Will Offend Some People

Well, that might be true, but as I (Glenn) stood before a congregation of over 500 people on a Sunday morning and had to tell them about their longtime administrator stealing over $250,000 during a five year period, that offended some people, too! So take your pick, possibly offending a few, or the entire church. Explain that you want to protect them *and* the church from even the appearance of evil!

> But examine everything carefully; hold fast to that
> which is good; abstain from every form of evil.
> 1 Thessalonians 5:21-22 (NASB)

If We Make Any Policy Changes, People Will Think Something Bad Just Happened

All three of us totally understand how people respond in churches. We have all been pastors and administrators of churches and other ministries. We all have served on ministry governing boards as well. All of us would rather take a bit of heat and discomfort for the sake of raising the standard at a ministry rather than stand by and watch it burn from lax procedures that lead to fraud. It is time to stand tall and lead in integrity and not simply to avoid possible conflicts. We must lead, not react.

It Really Does Not Matter That Much

If the true stories we have shared so far do not refute the above thought, we are not sure what will! It does matter, and it matters a great deal. Every time another Christian's integrity failure is flaunted on the front page of the newspaper or is the lead story on some news station, the larger Body of Christ is hurt.

Romans 2:24 reveals that our actions can encourage others to blaspheme our Lord Jesus Christ. When we fail in our handling of finances, morality, or integrity, we discredit the reality of the Gospel in our lives. As church leaders are led out of the buildings in handcuffs, or are shown confessing stealing money, or abusing those under their care, or violating their marriage vows, we all suffer a reputation hit for we are all part of the same Body.

The Church should be the leader in integrity in our community and we should be setting the standard of behavior, not the opposite. Our behavior in these situations matters a great deal and the ramifications reach to the farthest parts of the Church. We must do whatever is necessary to make sure that our local choices do not negatively impact every other church and ministry in the Kingdom.

"The Church Across Town"

In the last chapter, after a long-term administrator retired from "The Church Across Town," a trusted, long-term church member was hired to take his place as church administrator. What could be more safe and secure? Looking back, I think we violated nearly every myth listed in this chapter.

The single largest hurdle to bringing an end to the fraud was convincing leadership that an investigation was needed. In my opinion, as an outside consultant, this took the longest time.

In several discussions with Senior Pastor Bill, I would try to convince him that, while I did not have direct access to the data needed to prove fraud, I saw a pattern of behaviors and circumstances that often leads to fraud. It was not enough. Senior Pastor Bill stated:

Pastor Bill: And part of that was, I'm not the type of person who looks for a demon behind every bush. I'm going to assume the glass is half full. I just didn't think it was even a possibility that anyone would steal from a church. The church would have trusted the administrator because of his tenure here. He was a church member before I came on staff, they would have trusted him probably more than anyone on staff – including the pastor. And I, as the pastor, I trusted him, you know, without question. And so, I think it is wrong to trust without verification. I think verification is part of the responsibility process that *must* be put in place, regardless of where the trust factor is, high or low.

Another point we violated was to set policies and not enforce them for fear of offending anyone or drawing attention to potential shortcomings in our systems. Because of the serious nature of the church administrator's troubles outside of work, we felt horrible for even thinking about policies and procedures, much less implementing them, but we were wrong in thinking that. Senior Pastor Bill went on to state:

Pastor Bill: I think the risk of offending people is a risk worth taking. I think if you can make it a policy, if it can be part of the culture that "we verify." If we had, we would have stopped the fraud a lot sooner than we did.

Dear leaders of God's Church, it is time to clear up the illusions, debunk the myths, and stop making excuses that allow fraud to take place in our churches.

Action Questions

1. Are any of the myths on the list being used to justify a lack of action to combat fraud in your ministry?

2. How would you explain to your congregation that based on the myths presented, you and your leadership allowed the church to become a victim of fraud?

3. Does the money handling process leave your church vulnerable to fraud? How open is your church to changes that are needed to safeguard the church?

4. What changes need to happen at your church in order to make the necessary changes to begin the process of defeating potential fraud?

3 The Inconceivable Nature of Fraud

I was privileged to be a member of that church
for decades prior to me working there... ~Sam

A group of church leaders walked into the bank to sign the final papers for their new building loan. Finally, after years of fundraising, the down payment had been raised. All the hard work for those many long months, all the meetings, details, and effort were close to completion. Everyone was exited and couldn't wait to break ground on the much-needed new space. All that remained was to sign the note.

As the loan officer pushed the documents across the table towards the president of the counsel, soft sobs could be heard from the back of the group. A shaky voice said, "Don't sign it." Stomachs fell and fear began to clutch their hearts as everyone turned and stared at the source of the voice, the church treasurer. "Why on earth would you say such a thing?" he was asked. His reply, "There isn't any money, I spent it all. I have a girlfriend..."

Anger, betrayal, tears, and shock followed this untimely confession. Questions flooded the room and confusion reigned. The leaders began to pour out their angry inquiries:

- Where is the money?
- Why did you do this?
- How could you do this to us?
- What were you thinking?
- What are we going to tell everyone?
- Why did you wait until now to confess?

There were many more questions and more meetings, but you get the idea–the building was not going to be built anytime soon, and this church was in for a very stormy ride in the foreseeable future.

One question that provides some insight into the deception of fraud was this one – "Why did you wait until now to confess?" Why wait until you are in front of the loan officer to make this known? You knew there wasn't enough money, yet you let all of us make the trip and suffer the humiliation of this meeting. Why? These are perfectly normal questions.

The answer is not normal or even reasonable, but distorted deception is clearly evident.

"I kept praying for a miracle and hoping God would get me out of this mess."

The trusted treasurer, who was living in adultery, had stolen large sums of money to not only support his sin, but to hide it. He had hoped God would show up and make it all better in the final minute. The real miracle here is that after his revelation someone didn't do bodily harm to him when they left the bank!

How could someone who is a Christian, well known and respected, educated, and a member in good standing in their local church commit such a crime? While the answers are never easy, they are available. We will give you some of them in the chapter dealing with the Fraud Triangle, but for now, our point is that good people can, and often do, commit sinful actions. This is true even if we don't think they can or would.

While inconceivable to us, there simply are too many examples of good people who have made sinful choices in our day, and also throughout the Scriptures, to refute our claim.

- Adam sinned.
- Noah became drunk.
- Abraham lied about his wife.
- Who knows what Samson was thinking with Delilah?
- King David committed adultery, then murder to cover it up.

- Peter denied Christ three times and all the disciples fled.
- Multiple well-known pastors, TV evangelists, and famous authors have quit in shame. Okay, some have returned, but you get the idea.

Most of us probably know someone who was successful that ruined their ministry, family, and reputation by a sinful choice. Our initial reaction may have been, "I can't believe _____ did _____. Well, they did, and the fallout from their choices typically is harmful to far more than they ever imagined. More times than we could possibly know, people's faith is shaken and many questions arise in other churches as to their own policies and procedures. At least the last part of the previous sentence is helpful, for every church needs to review what they are doing and why in this area!

Many pastors, treasurers, leaders, and trusted bookkeepers have lied, cheated, stolen, and abused the people they were called to love, serve, and protect. Just saying it cannot happen will not prevent it or change the facts. It does happen, and far more often than we wish to admit.

On one financial consultation to a church, we shared our concerns for how their benevolent funds were being handled. They said "We've got that under control; we have two signatures on every check; we're good." I encouraged them to make some changes, but they refused.

Several years later they called us back for a suspicion of fraud in their benevolence fund account. Sadly, over $10,000 had been misappropriated for personal use over a several year period. The culprit used a very clever, intentional, well thought out scheme of writing the same check four times, using check signers on an exact rotating basis, so that no one would catch on to his pattern. He also used disappearing ink for the name on the check prior to garnering signatures and then later filled in his own name and cashed the checks. It is hard to believe that someone entrusted to help others with a benevolence fund would do this – but he did.

There are discernible reasons that people choose to lie, steal, commit adultery and fraud, and in the next chapter we will explore one of the best models explaining the cause. After gaining an understanding of this model, perhaps the word *inconceivable* will be changed into *inevitable* if we don't grow in our desire to help others in the area of integrity.

Case in Point

Mary had been church treasurer for over ten years and always did a great job doing the church's books on a volunteer basis. Unfortunately, the church was not aware of her gambling addiction. When her husband took appropriate steps at home to control the funds at her disposal, she then started using church funds. Over the next three years, Mary stole offering cash and went to the casino during the worship service to gamble. She also wrote checks to a company that she worked for who provided services to the church, overpaying invoices and taking that money to the casino as well. Mary was a professing Christian, wife, mother of two. Mary was a good church treasurer for the first seven years, but then things fell apart. How could this happen? The people of the church still have a hard time believing that it happened – but it did.

We could go on with other heart breaking examples and literally fill another hundred pages, but let's stop and check in on the continuing saga of:

"The Church Across Town"

As I placed more and more pressure on Administrator Sam, Pastor Bill and Treasurer Cindy they still had reservations. Because weeks had turned into months, I decided it was time to meet with Pastor Bill and Treasurer Cindy to see what needed to take place. When I explained that smoke is generally followed by fire, that I was seeing a lot of smoke, and that we needed to do a complete investigation, Treasurer Cindy, with great conviction and emotion put up her hand, stopping me symbolically, and said:

NO! Sam would never do this. He is a good family friend, and I refuse to believe what you are saying!

Pastor Bill responded: In the beginning I thought for sure, (or I wanted to believe) that it was just sloppy bookkeeping, poor skills, and lack of attention to detail. It's inconceivable to most people that someone who's on a church staff that they love, that they know, that they appreciate, would do anything like that. And so the idea of checking and verifying seems unnecessary, almost offensive. So we don't do it. And because we haven't done it, it's become unacceptable to do so. This has to change.

Later, Treasurer Cindy added: This individual is not only a friend, you know, but a close friend of the family. This is also someone who is fighting some real challenges outside of work. We just could not grasp that this person was stealing from the church.

Administrator Sam stated: I think we see that people who are in the ministry are treated differently than anybody else, really. And I don't mean that in a bad way, but in some ways I think we feel we put people up on maybe pedestals to a certain degree and so because you're staff in a church, you're not ever going to do anything wrong.

Just because we cannot conceive it, doesn't mean it can't happen. We must not be deluded into thinking that it cannot happen because of our optimism, care, concern, empathy or any other emotion that keeps us from seeing the truth.

Church, it's time to raise the standard!

Action Questions

1. What feelings, friendships, or alliances would keep you from embracing the possibility of fraud in your church?

2. What should be our attitude toward establishing policies and procedures?

3. What should our attitude be on trusting, but verifying?

4. Why do people steal from the church? (Continue reading to gain additional insight into this behavior and see if your answer lines up with ours.)

4 The Fraud Triangle

I mean it was always there, in everything I did.
It still was in the back of my mind,
I mean I knew that God...it was wrong. ~Sam

Pastors being led away in handcuffs, church staff members being fired for stealing, and administrators sneaking out of town due to financial mismanagement happen all too often. In fact, these things happen more than we might suspect. The news outlets gleefully share these stories, but in reality, in our experience, only one out of every five cases is exposed by the media. The enemies of Christ rejoice when Christian fraud is exposed, while the church or ministry suffers and many times slowly dies.

I (Glenn) remember working two different fraud cases that were also reported in the media. In both cases, the reporting was shoddy and woefully incomplete. While the perpetrator was usually identified correctly, the amount stolen and the methods used were grossly under reported. In one case, the local newspaper reported the church lost $100,000 and the actual amount was over $300,000. In another case, the reported loss was $60,000 and the actual amount was over $250,000. What does this reflect? The old adage is true – don't believe everything you read!

So how does this happen? Why are otherwise good, God fearing Christians from all walks of life lured into stealing from the church? Read on.

It has been said "no system is perfect or can prevent fraud 100%." While there are elements of truth in that statement, we can certainly learn the basics behind the behaviors and circumstances that can lead to fraud, and then work to prevent those circumstances.

In the 1940's, Donald Cressey of Indiana University did an extensive study of fraudulent behavior. Over seventy years later, his hypothesis is still considered to be a best model explaining occupational fraud via the Fraud Triangle.

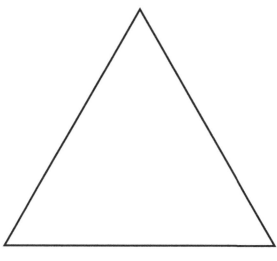

Perceived Opportunity

Pressure　　　　　　　　　　　　　*Rationalization*

It does not matter which direction you go, or at which point you start, each concept on the triangle: Perceived Opportunity, Pressure, and Rationalization, is important. According to Cressey's research, all three concepts were present in 97% of the cases he studied. In the cases of church fraud that we have encountered, 100% of the cases contained all three elements.

Pressure

Nearly all fraud cases involve some form or forms of outside pressure. Cressey labels this as an "un-shareable problem" where the perpetrator perceives that he/she cannot share the situation or problem with anyone because of social pressures: ego, shame, a perceived uncaring environment, or the inability to see how anyone can help. His phrase "un-sharable problem" is a very interesting concept that, while understandable in the secular world, should not be an issue in our church!

The treasurer that hoped for the last minute miracle believed that his problem was un-sharable, and apparently was not able, or did not feel comfortable, coming forward sooner.

Outside pressures are often related to financial situations. The following list comes from real life cases we have worked dealing with church fraud. Examples are:

- Living beyond means (golfing three days per week, expensive vacations, expensive cars, country club memberships, expensive home/homes)
- Too much debt (see above list of contributors!)
- Shopping addiction – online and in person
- Spouse's loss of income – layoff or other job loss
- Excessive medical bills
- Unpaid back taxes
- Gambling addiction
- Significant investment losses
- Living a double, deceitful life, i.e. supporting a second wife or girlfriend

While we, the church, cannot be held directly responsible for someone's outside pressures, we should always be on guard to help people in need and guide them to solutions that do not involve fraud. We must provide an atmosphere where those under external pressures can express their needs and find help within the church, instead of judgment that drives them away.

As pastors we need to be aware of the spiritual condition of those under our care. In the case of the small-town church in Chapter 2, the pastor found out that a member who handled the money had a gambling problem. Even though others had this knowledge, they did not connect the dots as it relates to pressure.

Relationships are needed, and communication is necessary, to provide insights into pressures that someone may be facing but unwilling to share freely. Asking questions and allowing the freedom to share difficulties may help prevent someone from choosing fraud. We cannot prevent people from sinning or cheating, but we should be able to assist those who really want to avoid it.

Rationalization

All sin begins in the mind, and fraud is no exception. The human mind is exceptional at rationalization. We can excuse almost any behavior in our lives through the power of reason and justification of ourselves. All fraud has at its base some form of rationalization. For example:

- The government doesn't spend my money correctly; therefore, I cheat on my taxes.
- The church does not reimburse me properly; therefore, I pad my expense account.
- The church does not pay me enough; therefore, I deserve this or that.
- My spouse does not meet my needs; therefore, I deserve to cheat on her/him.

We cannot recall the number of times (because it is so high) that we have worked with church staff, paid and volunteer, who has rationalized their fraud because they were over worked and underappreciated. In the case of the small-town church leader stealing cash, the spouse of the suspected embezzler was a faithful, but unpaid, volunteer in the worship ministry of the church.

Again, while the church is not responsible for the rationalizations people use to allow them to commit fraud, we should be teaching, preaching, and discipling people toward godly behaviors. God spoke to Cain before he murdered his brother and said,

> Sin is crouching at the door, and its desire is for you, but you must master it.
>
> Genesis 4:7 (NASB)

Christian people lie, cheat, steal, and then defend their behaviors with the power of rationalization. We must be on guard to listen for and take action upon such sentiments when we hear them. Once there is pressure building and someone begins the process of rationalization, then they are ripe for the last point on the pyramid.

Perceived Opportunity

The third aspect of fraud is the real or perceived opportunity to successfully complete the theft without getting caught. Every ministry is responsible for reducing, removing, or eliminating the real or perceived opportunity to get away with fraud. While we may not be responsible for outside pressures and/or rationalizations of individuals, we must create strong policies, procedures, and enforcements that keep honest people honest.

As Christians we do not want to live in the realm of suspicion. At the same time, we must set up policies and procedures that allow us to trust *and* verify. Most of the time, honest people are honest, and the vast majority of people who serve the Church do so from good motives. However, we must not tempt people with perceived opportunities, nor should we ignore the warning signs of pressure and rationalization. We want to trust, verify, and protect the church and its workers!

Let's check back and see how our brothers and sisters are doing as we follow the continuing story over at:

"The Church Across Town"

"The Church Across Town" had some good controls in place. They even had a few good policies and procedures, but lacked the knowledge and understanding of how to properly enforce and or verify that things were being done properly. So how did this fraud happen?

Perceived Opportunity

- Credit cards were used for personal gain. Paperwork and receipts were missing, and Administrator Sam did not have anyone checking his credit card bills.

- Administrator Sam had individual access to offering cash and was able to extract money undetected.

- Administrator Sam used one signature accounts payable checks to pay for personal items. Church policy required two signatures, but no one was checking.

- Administrator Sam took money each month from the church's PayPal account. He was not forced to show the reconciliation on the account, even though he was asked about it numerous times.

- Administrator Sam manipulated retirement contributions for his own personal gain. Again, no one was checking.

Does this list scare anyone besides the authors of this work? Yes, some policies were in place, but no regular or systematic checking or verifying took place.

Administrator Sam obviously perceived that he would be successful in his theft and took advantage of the church. Little did he know we saw the signs many months earlier and were getting closer and closer to proving it.

Administrator Sam: I think that as time went on, I think I got caught up in the ability to steal, I guess you would say, or the freedom that was there, in using some of that money.

But opportunity was not the only process at work; Sam also had outside pressures as well as rationalizations.

Outside Pressures
While we do not want to divulge the specifics of the outside pressures to protect the identity of Sam, they fell

into normal outside pressure categories that all of us face like:

- Multiple kids in private schools
- Major medical bills for several family members
- A failed business venture
- Major car repairs

The combination of these major categories and the inability and/or unwillingness to rapidly change and adjust, left Sam in a very pressing financial situation.

Rationalization

Sam's story clearly demonstrated using rationalizations.

Rationalization #1: "My intent was to pay it back." This is the most common rationalization in financial fraud. If you convince yourself you will pay it back, then you believe are not sinning, you are just borrowing out of temporary need.

Administrator Sam: And there were times where that did happen. Where I put money back in, into giving. So there was a little bit of...you know...well when I think back on it, there really was never very much of that money that was ending up going back.

The reality is, the stealing always gets worse, and money is rarely, if ever, actually repaid.

Rationalization #2: Overworked and underpaid. The church was struggling financially and as a result started to cut back staff. This added more work for those of who remained. In one stretch, staff members went several years without a raise.

Administrator Sam: You know, I was working a lot for the church and yeah you were feeling, or I was feeling, that I was working harder than what maybe I was being paid.

Rationalization #3: Overworked and underappreciated.

Administrator Sam: We were working long hours and I was on call 24/7 because of the building needs. It felt like I never really stopped working. I don't think people realized or fully appreciated how hard I worked, and so that helped me justify the church paying some of my bills.

Unfortunately, this is a very common problem in churches and ministries. It does NOT justify stealing, but it is a heavy contributor to rationalization.

Rationalization #4: I didn't really think I had taken that much. This is also a very common problem for fraudsters, especially Christians. We block out or try to forget in order to minimize the problem.

Administrator Sam: During the confrontation where everything was laid out, I was overwhelmed. One of the reasons I was so defensive is that I was having a hard time believing all of what I was seeing. The theft was much greater than I thought. There was no denying it; I was a thief. It was very difficult to cope with that reality.

Rationalization #5: The good things I've done far outweigh the bad. Sure I did some things wrong, the thinking goes, but I did a lot more good than I am given credit for.

Administrator Sam: I do think that in the everyday part of my job I guess I would say I had a good work ethic, but my ministry, I did have a ministry and it was very fervent and impactful, I think, over the years. You think about all the good things, you know, that we do, but yet when we come to a point of sinning before Jesus there is going to be some of those thoughts – I did not know you. So you kind of have a little bit of that. Not that I have any doubt that I'm a believer, that I'm saved.

You can see a clear path of rationalization that if we convince ourselves over a long enough time, it could lead to stealing from the church. Rationalization is one of the cleverest tools Satan has to lead us astray. Look back to the garden and the dialog of Adam and Eve with God!

The serpent asks Eve a question and in that instant plants seeds of distrust and rationalization:

So when the woman saw that the tree was good for food, and that it was a delight to the eyes, and that the tree was to be desired to make one wise, she took of its fruit and ate, and she also gave some to her husband who was with her, and he ate.

Genesis 3:6 (ESV)

We all know the story and the outcome. Rationalization was born and has been used by humans to excuse everything imaginable. Adam and Eve justified disobeying a simple, direct command from God Himself. Sam, and every other Christian who commits fraud, knows they should not steal. Yet, rationalization continues, and so does the death released by those sinful choices.

We must consider the truths contained in the Fraud Triangle and see how we can help others from following Adam, Eve, and Sam down the deadly path of sinful rationalization.

Action Questions

1. Think about a recent sin in your own life – how did you rationalize it?

2. Think about the last situation you were helping someone with who was dealing with sin. Were any of the three points of the Fraud Triangle involved in their battle?

3. What is your church responsible for? Rationalization, outside pressures, or perceived opportunity? Why?

4. What steps can your church take to do something about your answer in question 3?

5 Fire States: How Protected Is Your Ministry?

It's just hard. It was hard to know that I'd been, things were brought forth to me and I didn't really realize the magnification of it because I wasn't tracking it like you guys were tracking it. ~Sam

Today, the landscape of financial accountability in ministry has changed dramatically. Fraud in ministry is not new; it has been around for decades. What is changing is that in the past, fraud was less publicized in ministry because of the damage it would do to credibility and donations. In addition, most ministry boards are not set up or trained to handle this kind of breech in trust, so consequently, many fraud cases are covered up and not dealt with effectively. As more and more ministry fraud lands on the front pages of our local newspapers, and regulators and lawmakers become ever increasingly intolerant of people breaking the sacred public trust, increased accountability and scrutiny is quickly becoming the norm, not the exception.

We have looked at many of the illusions, myths, and excuses as to why churches refuse to change and lots of real life examples of why we should change. Many of the stories we have shared so far clearly illustrate how and why fraud took place in unsuspecting ministries. Now, it is time to move to self-evaluation and on toward solutions.

We have coined three categories, or states, that we found churches reside in to describe how well they are protected from fraud. We have used the analogy of fire because it seems to ring true to what is taking place in the church.

The vast majority of churches (up to 90%) fall into the first two categories: Fire Hazard and Fire Resistant. While the second state is more desirable than the first, neither is suitable for the Church of Jesus Christ, which should excel in financial integrity and reach the third state, Fireproof! These terms are not referring to the amount of old storage boxes and paint cans around the furnaces, but to the financial accounting and money management procedures a ministry uses which can leave them vulnerable to fraud.

Fire Hazard State

"An object, building, etc. that could easily catch fire or cause a fire and thereby endanger life."[2]

The Fire Hazard State is the most dangerous state in which a church can reside. Seventy percent of the churches where we perform an Administrative Audit reside in this state. It is defined as a relatively inactive, passive, trusting, and naive state regarding internal controls and the need to have policies and procedures to prevent fraud. Many ministries, especially high growth ministries, fail to keep up with the current business demands of their ministries and they simply settle into a passive routine.

Churches do not intentionally set themselves up to burn easily, yet this "hazard state" is where most ministries typically reside. It is a state that has been the standard operating model most likely since the ministry's inception. Many ministries are twenty, thirty, forty, or even fifty, or more years old. Things were different when the ministry began. The total focus was on ministering to people, as well it should have been. Money, finances, and accountabilities, much less fraud prevention, were all things that businesses needed to fuss with, not ministries. People were drawn to work in the ministry because of its vision and mission to help people, not because of the large salaries or opportunities to get rich.

We have shared numerous examples in earlier chapters; this passive, trusting state is not helping to stem the tide of negative publicity when a church member

---

[2] http://www.collinsdictionary.com/dictionary/english/fire-hazard

or staff person commits fraud. Fraud happens, and more than most of us would like to admit.

Most of us would not want to live in a house that was labeled a fire hazard. Yet, it seems that many are content to attend, give money to, and serve in a church that is financially living in a Fire Hazard State. Here we see clearly that a lack of knowledge and understanding on the part of leadership is leaving the church vulnerable. Perhaps ignorance is to blame, but that is no excuse. Donors are becoming more and more concerned over the proper handling of finances, and rightfully so!

Fire Resistant State

"The act or an instance of resisting, or the capacity to resist; a force that tends to oppose or retard." -Webster's Dictionary

The Fire Resistant State is an improvement to being in a Fire Hazard State, but still falls far short of what the goal should be – excellent integrity in all financial and personal matters. Our research indicates that approximately 20% of churches reside in this state.

The Resistant State, as defined as by Webster's Dictionary is "The act or an instance of resisting, or the capacity to resist; a force that tends to oppose or retard."

While we agree the Resistant State is an upgrade from being in the Hazard State, the Resistant State is reactionary, multifaceted in its origins, and is commonly driven by current and/or past circumstances and/or current needs. It tends to behave in a "discover and then react" mode. Systems are designed to discover and then react to issues or needs "after the fact." Examples include:

- A local ministry was on the six o'clock news; we better take action before we are!
- Ten years ago, we had a staff member that committed fraud, so we need to do this or that to prevent another occurrence.
- An angry church member (or former one) accused us of "X", therefore we better do "Y."
- Fraud has happened and we must react or we will lose our large donors.
- We now have a CPA on our board, so we better straighten up our policies.
- We are getting ready to start a new capital campaign, or annual pledge drive, or apply for new funding, so we better get our financial house in order.

The problem with this state is that it appears to be just what it is: *reactionary*, after the fact, knee jerk, operating in an uninformed state, poor leadership, and at best, poor management/stewardship.

Operating in this state for any length of time or repeated instances where it even "appears" that you are operating in this state regularly, can leave a lasting impression on your constituents that can significantly reduce your ministry's effectiveness, and perhaps it should.

While the reasoning in this stage is not all bad, this reactionary state will not answer the correct questions nor lead in the proper direction of change necessary to live in the Fireproof State.

This Fire Resistant State is driven by, or born from, a reaction, not a purposeful, well thought out set of financial integrity goals. It is driven by either internal or external factors and will lead to multiple knee jerk reactions and band-aid fixes, depending on the size and scope of the issues encountered.

Fireproof State

"Resistant to destruction by fire; totally or almost totally unburnable." This is the typical understanding of the term.

The Fireproof State of financial accountability should be the desired state for all ministries. 1 Thessalonians 5:21-22 clearly defines our objective in this state:

Prove all things; hold fast to that which is good.
Abstain from all appearance of evil. (KJV)

Proactive processes and procedures mark this state. It is intended to prevent, rather than discover and react to fraud. Characteristics of this state include:

- Clear goals regarding level of financial integrity to achieve
- Clear expectations as to what that will take
- Good communications
- Strong policies and procedures

- Proactive training
- Checks and balances and verification
- Appropriate levels of auditing

Ministries are a lot like trees. It is widely understood that a tree without a strong and healthy root system will not withstand the perils of drought, high winds, and other natural forces that can come against trees. The more fertile the ground is, the stronger the root system, the healthier the tree, and the bigger the fruit.

Good administration and strong financial accountabilities are often behind the scenes or underneath the surface, but they play a *vital* role in a healthy root system.

The Beginning of Change

So how does a church find out which state it is in? We have included a detailed assessment in the Appendix section of this book.

We recommend (and hereby give you permission) copying the assessment and having the leadership team, the church council, the staff, the finance team, the audit committee, and whoever else needs to, assess and/or learn about the topic and take the assessment. The results you will find might amaze you. They typically include:

- We are much more vulnerable than we anticipated.
- People across the congregation see things very differently.
- We really need to make some changes immediately.
- We really need to do some training.

The assessment, or checklist, is broken down into three columns: Fire Hazard, Fire Resistant, and Fireproof. As you read down the left column, you will find the area of financial integrity being addressed, such as Check Signing or Payroll details. Moving across the top of the chart will be the three states possible for each area and what typically occurs in them.

By reading across the chart, you can see where your organization is in the process. At the end of the checklist is a self-evaluation, or grade, for your group. Be honest, and then look at what you need to do to move 100% to the Fireproof State!

If your ministry's score is not very high, don't be overly discouraged. That just means improvement will happen quickly when you do implement change! Almost every ministry needs to improve, and if yours does not, then congratulations, you are in a very small minority! Your donors should feel very relaxed and so should you.

Some have asked us, "Do we really need all of these controls to be fireproof? Isn't this a bit of overkill?" Well, perhaps a picture will help make our point. It is all about layers of protection. I can go outside in 30-degree weather and be just fine, for a while. But if we think about additional controls as layers of protection, then they make more sense. If I put on a tee shirt, then a regular shirt, then a sweater, and then an overcoat with gloves and a hat and proper snow boots, I can be relatively certain I am going to be protected from the harms of cold weather. If I refuse to add layers of protection, eventually becoming cold, perhaps frostbite, or even death is a possibility.

We mentioned earlier that most people would not willingly choose to live in a house that is a fire hazard. Do you want to live in a house with your children where the house is "kind of ok" with regard to security? Do you want to live in a house where "most of the windows lock? Half of the outside doors close properly? The garage door is "mostly closed?"

The more controls you have in place, the safer and more secure your church will become.

Brothers and sisters in Christ, it is time to help keep the Bride of Christ safer! Before moving on into the next chapter, let's check in with...

"The Church Across Town"

Pastor Bill: There is no doubt we needed more controls in place. We had "some" good policies and procedures, and that lead us to believe we were "ok," when clearly we were not.

Churches need to create good policies and procedures but they also must create a culture that states clearly, "We will be checking to keep honest people honest."

Pastor Bill: Now, it was hurtful to be that trusting. You know, trust but verify. It had to happen. And how it happened is imperative. And I think if we don't check, it's almost a guarantee it's going to happen. If people know...if the policies are sloppy...it's not a question of will it happen, it's just when it will happen. Because I think it's a temptation that is probably too great for most people.

Treasurer Cindy: We had some good controls in place and we have added additional policies and procedures and tightened up others that were a bit loose. The key thing we missed was checking and verifying instead of trusting good Christian people who was also a close friend. Our trust and friendship kept me from seeing what was happening. It was and still is very painful to think about.

Action Questions:

1. Take the assessment in the Appendix yourself. What is the score? How do you feel about where your church is?

2. Have your staff or key leaders take the assessment. How does their score line up with yours? What is the difference and why?

3. Is change needed? Why or why not?

4. Who will be responsible for the changes necessary?

6 Fireproofing Your Ministry

But I mean, really looking at everything that we have that could be temptations for people. ~Sam

As we learned in the chapter on the Fraud Triangle, whenever fraud takes place, it is at least partially due to the real or perceived opportunity to get away with the crime. Logic would dictate that if we could limit the real or perceived opportunity, we could significantly reduce the instances of fraud. While many of the following items are, or should be, obvious, most churches are not implementing them, or sticking to them, so they bear repeating.

As you looked through the Fireproof column in the checklist in the Appendix, there were probably some areas that needed attention in order to strengthen your financial integrity and limit fraud opportunities. Some would argue that it costs too much to implement change, or that it will be too time consuming. We would stress that there may be some cost of time and money involved, but that cost is certainly far less than the damage caused by fraud.

Let's look at some no to low-cost changes that can be made.

Cash Receipts

Every ministry receives money. Who handles it, who counts it, and how it is deposited and reported will help determine how safe the ministry is. Here are some no to low-cost guidelines to implement:

- Money should always be counted by at least two people. Three are better.
- Checks received in the mail should be opened in the presence of two people.
- Both counters should sign off on the final count sheet.
- Both counters should count cash independently.
- Money counters should rotate to limit the possibility of collusion.
- Counters should not be related.

- All checks should be immediately endorsed with a deposit stamp.
- A duplicate deposit slip should be made out at the time of counting, one copy is deposited, and the other is given to the bookkeeper/accountant. These two deposit slips should never be together until after the deposit is made, thus limiting the opportunity for changing the original deposit.
- The bookkeeper/accountant matches the deposit slip processed by the bank to the contribution database and the General Ledger each month.
- Written instructions are provided explaining exactly what is expected.

If a ministry does all of those steps above, opportunities for fraud will be greatly reduced. The actual out-of-pocket expense for the ministry so far is zero!

Cash Disbursements

If a ministry receives any donations, they will eventually spend them. A great deal of fraud takes place during this spending process, but it can be prevented with good controls.

- Two signatures required on every check. A signature stamp does not count and will not limit fraud. This technique is for the church, not the bank.
- Supporting documentation for every check, *prior* to signing the check, no exceptions.

- Check signers are not related and not in a direct supervisor/subordinate relationship if at all possible.
- Blank checks are never signed. *Ever.*
- The same person who generates the check does not sign the check. At least one of the check signers signs all the checks to look for reoccurring patterns.
- Employee reimbursements are made only *after* receiving proper documentation. Petty cash funds should be avoided.
- If credit cards are used, documentation is required for every purchase and is examined by someone other than the user of the credit card. Debit cards should be avoided.
- Voided checks are clearly marked "VOID," and the signature section is cut off. They are stored in a secure location, never thrown out.
- Someone reviews bank statements other than the one who writes or signs the checks. Even better is to have the bank statement mailed to someone else's location outside of the organization for review.

If a ministry will follow these steps for spending within the organization, the opportunities for fraud will be severely limited. The actual out-of-pocket expense for the ministry so far still remains at zero!

Payroll

Since most ministries will hire employees, it is essential that they follow wise and legal procedures. As recent headlines have shown, the IRS is not overly friendly towards Christian groups, so great care is needed.

- All compensation changes need to be approved by someone other than the employee and must include appropriate documentation.
- All compensation, including love offerings, special gifts, and bonuses must be processed through the approved payroll system. No choice; this is the IRS standard.
- A current W-4 and I-9 is on file for every employee.
- The correct usage of W-2 vs. 1099's is critical.
- The appropriate people approve housing allowances for those that qualify before the current year begins.
- All applicable wage and hour guidelines, employee classification, and overtime laws are followed.
- All payroll taxes and the required reports are filed in a timely fashion according to the current laws for federal, state, and local jurisdictions.

The IRS is serious about enforcement. Many ministries have been audited and fined for failure to follow the above procedures. While there may be a cost to the ministry to begin to obey the law, this cost is minimal compared to the fines and bad press received if the ministry fails to do so.

Bank/Investment Accounts and Financial Statements

Unless the ministry keeps its funds strictly in cash (humor), financial institutions will be involved. Banks and other investment and financial firms issue statements to their customers. The following procedures will provide an additional layer of protection to the ministry.

- A minimum number of bank accounts are used and are balanced to the penny monthly.
- These balances must tie into the General Ledger and the contribution statements.
- Someone other than the person creating the checks should review and balance the statements.
- Strict, generally accepted accounting procedures should be used to reconcile and report to the appropriate committees responsible for the funds.
- Financial statements should be timely (each month) and complete and again follow generally acceptable accounting procedures.
- Financial statements must include a balance sheet (Statement of Financial Position) and an income statement (Statement of Activities).
- A person, or preferably a committee, should review the statements each month and ask appropriate questions!

All of the above procedures have a relatively low cost to the ministry. Compared to the expense and devastation caused by fraud, the cost represents perhaps one of the church's best return on investment opportunities they will have, financially speaking. Any ministry can implement these guidelines and should. We as Christians should hold to the highest standards in our handling of money and never settle for anything less.

In addition to the above steps, there are a few other issues to be considered when pursing the Fireproof State:

- Consider an annual audit, discussed fully in a Chapter 8.
- If at all possible, try to have a wise, experienced, competent financial officer or treasurer on your board. Someone who understands accounting, but more importantly, church accounting, is very helpful.
- Consider hiring an outside firm to assist with accounting, payroll, and human resources to assure accuracy, add a measure of separation of duties, and a third party reviewing your transactions.
- Also consider an annual fraud risk assessment by an outside group and preferably a Certified Fraud Examiner.
- Approve an anti-fraud policy for the church and make sure all employees know it. Include an "intent to prosecute" clause to communicate the seriousness of the issue.

Even with all of the above in place, we can never eliminate every opportunity of theft or fraud, but we can certainly take these steps to help limit the opportunities and temptations. We can leave our front door open when we go on vacation and just hope all is well, or we can install a deadbolt. We can remove the paint cans and boxes from the open flame by our furnace, or just pray they do not explode. As in so many other areas of our life, the choice is ours. Choose wisely.

Even the smallest, least staffed ministry can implement most of the suggestions in this chapter, and we would argue that they should, that is, if they want to avoid fraud and maintain an excellent financial reputation.

Church leaders, remember – people will use our behavior as a benchmark or an excuse. Let's be a benchmark for financial integrity!

Before moving on into the next chapter, let's check back in with:

"The Church Across Town"

As you can see from the chapter checklist and from comparing that to the areas where Administrator Sam was able to steal money from his church, the policies clearly needed updating. Even enforcement of the policies they did have would have made a big difference.

Oftentimes we hire or enlist a volunteer administrator or bookkeeper or accountant because of their skill and their tendency to do things right. We expect these people to enforce the rules and keep staff and well-meaning volunteers in line and in compliance with good financial practices. And, while that is a fair expectation, the truth is, competent, trustworthy people are the ones committing most of the fraud! We must help our brothers and sisters in positions of authority to stay accountable and protected. We must trust and verify.

Treasurer Cindy: For the longest time I thought for sure; not this person. In looking back, the administrator job got handed off by a gentleman that had been doing it for years when I first came on to the stewardship committee, you know a great guy. But it was done on a piece of paper or a napkin, and it never grew up. It never matured.

That sort of allowed the administrator to...well...it allowed this to happen. Because if we would had run our books like a bigger church, if you will, had more firewalls, more things in place, more people checking, you know, more checks and balances, it probably could have been prevented.

Pastor Bill: I assumed it was another staff member other than the administrator. So I kept putting the responsibility on him to get it from others. I wish at that point I would have known who it was – specifically because I had jumped to a conclusion that it was others.

Action Questions

1. What is your reaction to the ideas presented in this chapter? Why?

2. What would it take for your ministry to implement the suggested changes in this chapter?

3. Is there any good reason (not an excuse) why these changes cannot be implemented?

4. Who could be your point person to begin a review and implementation process?

7 The Role of Internal Controls

And I don't mean necessarily that you walk into every church and say that there is somebody going to be tempted, but if there is, like unchecked credit cards,... because that's an easy one. ~Sam

Control seems to be a negative word in our day. Many are placing freedom and control in opposition to one another. While there may be some validity in this argument when arguing law verses grace, there is not as much gray area when dealing with financial accountability. Most of the real life stories we have shared with you about church fraud could have been avoided with a simple set of internal controls and proper follow through.

Controls are valuable and all around us in our daily life. Just consider what society would be like without them and the prospect is frightening. Looting, violence, and rioting have taken place when law enforcement control has been abandoned. What is a computer virus but a program running out of control? Stoplights, passwords, painted lines on the highway; are all controls. Would we wish they were not there? If you have driven a car in a third world country, you already know the answer! Controls are necessary and good. This is especially true when dealing with the finances of a ministry.

First things first – establish the *purpose* of your financial guidelines, policies, and procedures. Answer the why question early and policy formation will be a much smoother ride. All good policy should be ministry driven. That is to say, every policy should help, protect, and otherwise enhance the ministry's ability to reach its God-given mission. Also embedded in that definition is an implied concept of not "over" managing and controlling.

Case in Point

I (Glenn) was asked to meet with a finance committee of a local church and help them trouble shoot some issues they had with their finances. I attended a 1.5 hour finance committee meeting followed by a 2.5 hour business meeting. In the business meeting, they were voting on and approving each expenditure of the church over $100.00. This was a time consuming and tedious task. At one point, the meeting got so contentious that a motion was passed stating that every six minutes they would stop and pray to help calm people down. And that is what they did.

After the meeting, I met again with the finance committee and they asked "So, what do you think?" I looked around the room to see if anyone was smiling, or if everyone was serious, trying to discern if they were joking or not. I asked them if they wanted me to speak candidly, without sugar coating anything. They agreed.

- I asked them if they had a church approved annual budget, and the answer was yes, they did.
- I asked them if the budget had specific line items in it for each department. Again, the answer was yes.
- I asked them why they voted on each expenditure over $100.00. They told me that seventeen years ago, Pastor Jim stole some money from the church and they vowed to never let that happen again!

After further research, I found that most of the church bills were now under $100.00. There were two invoices for paper, $90.00 each, in sequential order, obliviously ordered at the same time, but just under the approval wire! While effective in circumventing the need for approval, this system was not effective. This is a clear case of over managing to prevent fraud. Set up accountable systems that are easy to manage and easy to verify. Don't overdo it! What this church needed were accountabilities, not additional controls.

Every church should establish internal controls as soon as possible, beginning with the goals of the process. The pastor and leaders need to dialog and think through how they will conduct the personnel and financial business of the ministry.

Procedures should be written and reviewed on a regular basis to make sure the highest integrity possible is being achieved. We love the way the KJV translates 1 Thessalonians 5:22 – "Abstain from all appearance of evil." We are not to even look like we are doing anything wrong to someone observing us. Internal controls can help!

If the person counting the offering places the money in his pocket while someone is watching, what do we think the other person will think? If the pastor and a woman, not his wife, are over in a dark corner embracing, what will someone observing think? People are watching, and jumping to wrong conclusions is a favorite occupation of some people.

We cannot always prevent people from their negative way of thinking, but we can certainly not give them more fuel for the fire. We must be aware and we must be careful.

Every ministry must think through what they want to communicate to others by their actions. The way we collect money, spend it, and report it speaks to the financial integrity of our group. The way we conduct ourselves around the opposite sex will reflect our stands on sensuality, immorality, and moral purity. We must be careful to assure that what we are giving an "appearance of" is what we are intending.

Internal controls also help with communication and expectations within our ministries. If we do not have any written guidelines, then how will those who work with us know our standards and expectations? How can we instruct, correct, or applaud behavior when those who work with us must simply guess what we want from them?

We would suggest that you write out your internal controls in at least these areas to help protect your ministry:

- Ethics and general conduct
- Inter-personal relationships and behaviors
- Social media
- Cash receipts
- Cash disbursements
- Reimbursements
- Work schedules, service attendance, vacation/sick days, reviews
- Ministry property usage
- Intellectual property rights while working
- Dress codes and personal appearance
- Personal business while at the office
- Others?

Every ministry will be different and that is good. However, we all should strive to excel in integrity and not have even an appearance of evil in any fashion. The enemies of Christ are always looking for our flaws, and while we will always have them, we must not be casual or careless about them, but seek to strengthen and correct them.

Leaders of the church, it starts with us! A CPA friend and colleague, John Parrish, emphasizes that "Tone at the Top" will determine how others in your organization will act and carry out their duties.

Let's set a high bar for integrity and then walk it out! Before moving on to discuss the role of audits, let's check back with:

"The Church Across Town"

Pastor Bill: I once served at a church where my integrity was tested in the very first week. The administrator and I were out shopping at an office supply store getting things for my new office. Innocent enough. At one point, he said, "Hey, come over here to the computer section. You really need this. In fact, as senior pastor, you deserve this!" He was holding up the latest and greatest and most expensive notebook of that time. I clearly didn't need that and I said, "No, that really isn't a need at this point." It was a set up for failure! Had I gone along with his theory of "need and deserving," what else would that have led to? Found out later that there was a pattern of indulging on staff that was not of God.

In "The Church Across Town" I was also tested early on. Several staff members took liberties with purchases that were not appropriate. It cost me a great deal of capital with my congregation to put a stop to excess spending. It was a hard road and cost me dearly, but I could not let that happen under my watch.

Action Questions

1. If you haven't thought about internal controls before, what are the advantages of having them? Any disadvantages?

2. How can addressing the issues of financial integrity help your ministry? Explain.

3. In the ministry, can you draw a line between personal and ministry behavior? Explain.

4. Who in your church might be able to help you with this project?

8 The Role of Audits

*I think it would be very worthwhile for a church
to have that audit piece. And not just an overall audit
of saying, you know, on about the 10,000-foot level
saying, yeah this is fine.* ~Sam

Our purpose for this chapter is to explain the necessity for outside review to maintain or achieve a Fireproof State for our ministry.

Does hiring an auditor automatically prevent fraud? What do audits cost and who should do them? Does every church need an annual audit? What is the difference between a full-blown audit and a review? Do we have to hire a CPA firm to achieve our goals, or is there some other way? Does it matter?

We have included a detailed explanation of the various types of services offered by a typical CPA firm in the appendix of this book. For this chapter, we offer the following general summary: first and foremost, we strongly recommend obtaining any audit services desired from an accounting firm that specializes in churches/Christian ministries. Prices vary greatly depending on frequency and the exact type of audit needed. Here are four basic types of industry offerings:

1) A public accounting firm and a CPA firm can both offer what is referred to as a *compilation*. This is a summary of all known accounting transactions as provided by the client. It has no assurance as it represents only what the client has provided.

2) A *review* can only be provided by a CPA firm. It typically includes a compilation plus additional scrutiny of records that make up the financial statements of the church. It has a higher level of assurance than the compilation the CPA will make specific inquiries of management and apply analytical procedures to unusual items or trends that may need explanation.

3) A *full or certified audit* can only be provided by a CPA firm. It offers the highest level of assurance based on more extensive testing. It also provides

more detailed reports, comments, and recommendations.

4) An *administrative procedures audit* has been developed by my firm, Miller Management Systems, LLC, specifically designed for churches seeking to have a complete review of all financial practices in the church. It provides the latest best practices in the industry and an implementation planner to help churches through the process of making needed changes. It also includes a compilation.

Shopping for the best price is mandatory, but before you shop for an audit service and firm, make sure you understand your goals and reasons for the services hired.

Important note: Audits are not designed to discover or prevent fraud. This is a common misunderstanding. Even an unqualified opinion (which is the goal for a full audit) does not mean fraud is not happening! It only means "there is a reasonable assurance based on testing and procedures purported to be in place, that no material fraud is taking place." Further, according to the AICP, the national CPA governing body, only 11% of fraud is caught by external auditors.

Case in Point

I (Glenn) was working at my first church administration job while working on my MBA. After a couple of years at the church, I was recruited to be the controller at a well-known seminary in our city. What an opportunity for a 29-year-old, fresh out of MBA school! Looking back, I sometimes wonder if that is the real reason he hired me, because I was young and inexperienced!

Only about two years into the position, I discovered a pattern of suspicious behavior. Not yet a Certified Fraud Examiner, I did seem to have a nose for this sort of thing. What I discovered was that my boss, (and friend, colleague, Christian, school board member, deacon in the local church,) was stealing from the seminary. It was a pattern of stealing that started very small and grew to tens of thousands of dollars over a seven-year period.

But how can this be? We had a full annual CPA audit every year as was required by our accreditation bodies. We eventually discovered that this person was a former Federal Reserve auditor who knew just how to manipulate things to get around auditors' checks.

Bottom line regarding audits is to know what you want/need and understand what you are purchasing. Simply spending money for an audit may provide some emotional security, but might not be the best use of funds.

That said, we still strongly recommend getting some outside, professional, industry specific help. One obvious advantage of hiring or using an outside group is objectivity. A fresh set of eyes looking over our procedures, policies, and actual practices is helpful. Every ministry slips into a comfortable routine and a new perspective can catch oversights we may have missed.

Along with objectivity is the anticipation and expectation that the outside people will ask questions, and lots of them. They are generally not afraid of political or emotional lines that at times prevent us from asking tough questions.

In general terms, what will be, or should be, reviewed, typically consists of the following tasks included in the Miller Management Systems, LLC, scope of work:

- General Accounting – Assess General Ledger transaction, financial reports, and general compliance issues relating to the reporting of data.

- Budget Process – Evaluate the budget process and corresponding financial reporting confirming that the record keeping is in balance with the intent of the budget process.

- Incoming Funds – Evaluate all areas associated with the receiving and handling of funds including processes, internal controls, and workflow. As applicable, review contribution statement accuracy through verification letters to a sample of contributors, and observe an offering counting process.

- Disbursement of Funds – Evaluate all areas and processes associated with the retention and disbursement of funds. This includes analyzing check processing procedures, verifying documentation for a sample of payments, and reviewing bank statements.

- Payroll/Payroll Taxes – Evaluate the payroll process and related tax filings to ensure compliance and accuracy. This includes a review of staff compensation and general human resource policies and administration.

- Personnel – Evaluate processes, procedures, and documents related to handling of personnel within the organization.

- Compare insurance coverage to industry standards.

- Review basic Information Technology structure.

Preparation Is the Key

In order to get ready for an audit, regardless of who you use, the following tips will help keep your records in great shape:

- Attach the check stub to the invoice or check request.

- Be consistent with how you file documents (e.g. John Smith, owner and sole employee for ABC Lawn Mowing, may be under J, S, A, or L).

- Include the who, what, when, where and why on documentation for meal receipts.

- Whenever there is responsibility associated with correct data or approval on documents, forms; include a signature (e.g. offering counting documentation, time sheets, expense reimbursement approvals).

- As a default, use a signature rather than initials.

- Avoid signature stamps unless under lock and key of the individual whose signature is on the stamp, OR better yet, never use them!

- When ensuring appropriate approvals for expense reimbursements, have the person responsible for that department's expenses sign.

- Ensure that you have an annual review of signature cards for each bank account.

- Know your credit card limits and limit them to actual need.

- Close credit cards and vendor accounts no longer used.

- Keep documentation of all key holders and combination holders.

- Ensure the accounts payable and accounts receivable sub ledgers balance to the General Ledger prior to the final day of the fiscal year.

- Make documentation clear to those not involved in creating it.

- All bank accounts should be reconciled monthly, with printed reconciliations attached to the related bank statement.

- Balance all quarterly and annual payroll taxes – W-2s, 941s, etc.

Here are some CPA General Accepted Accounting Practices that, if followed, will help your ministry in its pursuit of financial excellence:

- Annually, have someone other than the originator of the financial spreadsheet(s) check all formulas and calculations for accuracy.

- Annually, assess risk of fraud with board, leadership and staff (see ACFE website).

- Provide all board, leadership, and staff with annual anti-fraud training.

- Prepare and maintain a GAAP depreciation schedule for all physical plant assets and equipment and make year-end entries to that effect.

- Based on a handbook policy, make entry for accrued vacation or sick pay, or any other accrued benefits, including payroll, prior to the close of the year.

- Have in place an AICPA-approved whistle-blower, anti-fraud, and conflict of interest policy (see Appendix).

- In general, new regulations prohibit auditors from significant cleanup, rearrangement, or otherwise making material alterations to financial statements. Be sure that all estimates, journal entries, accruals, and other financial statement adjustments are made prior to the close of the final month of the year. If estimates are used, they need to be as accurate as possible, supported by rationale and documentation.

Most auditors will tell you that simply having an audit will not prevent, or in some cases, even reveal fraud. However, having an outside, qualified person or team review the financial statements, your policies, and procedures, will greatly enhance the chances of discovering or discouraging it. If everyone knows that the ministry is going to be audited, that alone can often deter fraud.

Additionally, given the all too frequent negative press of ministries that have had suffered some sort of fraud, adding this layer of protection will enhance your image with both your donors and the community.

So, did "The Church Across Town" have audits?

"The Church Across Town"

Administrator Sam: If there is a way to have somebody else do the actual accounting part of what you're submitted. I mean we submitted accountability sheets on those, reconciliation sheets, but you have to have one card maybe. Or, you know, something to where then those pieces would be very evident if they weren't fitting together. So an accountability piece.

Treasurer Cindy: Church size is, to me, is a relative matter. I mean, you can have a pretty large body of givers and attendees, but to me, it's how the church is ran. If you get a church that ran as a small shop, in a mom-and-pop way – and that was one of our problems.

Pastor Bill: And going back, one of the things that I would do is not only to make sure that the credit cards balance, but to literally...I think the church should go back on an annual basis and do an evaluation. Even a quick evaluation of, "Does the amount of credit card expenditure, or expenditures within the ministry, line up with what we wanted?

Sadly, "The Church Across Town" had periodic audits and/or reviews, not every year, but several over a period of years. We do not blame the CPA firm because finding fraud is not their job. But unfortunately, because of a lack of knowledge and understanding, sometimes leaders have been heard saying, "We had an annual audit, we are good!" It is as if they use the annual audit as an excuse not to do their own due diligence. Don't let this happen to your church!

Action Questions

1. After considering the role of an audit for your ministry, what would you recommend to your church? Why?

2. What would be some advantages to having a regular audit?

3. What would prevent your church from having some form of external audit?

4. As you read through the various points in this chapter, which ones stood out to you as the most necessary?
   Why?

9 When Fire Breaks Out

And I mean by the law's standards, restitution
should be made with, you know, dollar for dollar.
But yet, there is also that piece of the relationship
that you have and that trust that you have,
that you've broken, but yet, it's still there. ~Sam

The worst fears have been realized and the trusted bookkeeper, treasurer, or beloved pastor has turned out to be guilty of the grievous sin of fraud. What do we do now? What will everyone think when they find out? What will happen to our beloved ministry when all of this becomes public? What a mess...

Just like a trained firefighting professional approaches a burning building, we must not over or under react to the discovery of fraud.

While an oversimplification, the ministry is often comprised of two main groups of people regarding how to deal with the offender – on the one hand; you have those who want to extend grace, mercy, and are concerned for the well being of the guilty person and their family. "After all," they say, "Didn't Jesus say it is more blessed to forgive? Let's just forgive and move on." On the other hand, there will be people who lean more towards the, "Let's hang them!" approach. "If we wink at sin, the Kingdom will be destroyed! We must take a stand for righteousness!" Oddly enough, we rarely find people who are in the middle; it is usually a very polarizing event in the church.

The truth is they are both right. There are tensions that run throughout the Scriptures and it is often unclear which side of the argument we should stand upon. We are to forgive, but we are not to ignore sin. We are not supposed to judge, and yet we are called to be fruit inspectors. We must extend grace to those who fail, for whom among us has not? We are to help hold people accountable, but always with an eye towards redemption, not condemnation.

There are no perfect answers to life's messy questions at times – and this is one of those times. What follows are some basic guidelines that we have developed from our experiences of what has worked, as well as what has not worked. This is how we suggest you attempt to walk through the fire, hopefully extinguish it, and then in the next chapter, how to move on into the future.

1. If you suspect fraud might be happening, *do not approach the individual suspected*, but gather the facts. Be sure you collect the correct facts. Most people only confess when confronted or cornered with the facts.

   ✓ Look for changes in behavior or changes in circumstances, inside or outside of work.
   ✓ Look at internal control weaknesses and see if fraud is possible.
   ✓ Look at documentation, establish a trail if possible, and review records before and after suspected fraudulent activity.
   ✓ Carefully interview people with knowledge, preferably not leading them to conclusions.
   ✓ Document everything possible or within reason.
   ✓ If it looks to be a serious situation, or too complex, hire outside help:
     • A Certified Fraud Examiner
     • An outside accounting firm
     • Possibly law enforcement depending on the circumstance

2. If there is *little or no direct proof of fraud*, consider a change in accounting control to prevent what you suspect. Watch closely in the future.

Speaking of tensions; there is a difference between suspicion and observation. We want to walk in the realm of trusting people; however we do not want to be foolish. "Trust but verify" is a wise sentence. If the changes implemented prove to prevent fraud, wonderful! If not, then move on to the next step.

This was the process employed by the small-town church in Chapter 2. Outside of adding surveillance cameras to obtain direct proof, it was going to be hard to prove wrongdoing. The change in accounting controls related to the offering resulted in the desired outcome (and additional income!)

3. **If fraud is discovered with** *direct or indirect evidence,* **proceed with caution.**

   ✓ *If it is "minor" fraud* defined as small amounts over a short period of time, less than a couple of months, items like: credit card misuse, taking of small assets for personal use, charging personal items to ministry vendor accounts, falsifying time cards or mileage reimbursements, etc.

Perhaps a Mathew 18 encounter is warranted. Go to them at an appropriate time, with a reliable witness, show them what areas you have concerns over, ask them direct questions, and go from there. If dealt with at this level, a major breach of trust and damage to the ministry can possibly be avoided. However...

   ✓ *If it is more pronounced, intentional,* and of medium length—six months or more, more than $1,000, multiple incidents:
   • Consider getting outside legal assistance.
   • Hire a Certified Fraud Examiner.
   • Hire an outside accounting firm.

- Consider law enforcement assistance.
- Have an audit performed by an external firm and share your concerns with the audit firm.
- Consider immediate removal or isolation from areas of fraud to protect the person and the ministry, or a paid or unpaid leave of absence until size and scope can be measured.
- Create a workable game plan, execute the plan, and stick with it.
- Consider reviewing insurance coverage to ensure that it remains intact.

✓ *If it is major fraud*, for an extended period of time—more than a year, more than $5,000, multiple incidents:
- Get outside legal assistance immediately.
- Hire a Certified Fraud Examiner and outside accounting firm.
- Strongly consider law enforcement assistance.
- Have an audit performed by an external firm and share your concerns with the audit firm.
- Implement immediate removal or isolation from areas of fraud to protect them and the ministry, or a paid or unpaid leave of absence until size and scope can be measured.
- Contact insurance company to determine liability coverage and requirements of the insurance company.
- Create a workable game plan, execute the plan, and stick with it.

If major fraud has taken place, it is past time to worry about hurting someone's feelings by exposing it.

Relationship damage will probably take place, but this is minor compared to arrests and destroyed reputations. If the relationship can be salvaged, wonderful, but if not, then the overall reputation of the ministry must take precedence.

There are greater issues involved than just your ministry and relationships when sin breaks out. The enemies of Christ rejoice, the media loves to point out the hypocrisy, and many believers are ultimately hurt. We must walk in integrity and we must deal with these sinful issues.

A wise pastor once said:

Always do what is right. People are going to be upset about something no matter what you do, so always do the right thing, and then people will be upset with you for the right reasons.

We as leaders must be willing to put the interests of the Kingdom and Jesus' Church before our own. If someone has violated the law, stolen money, committed adultery, or any sin against the Church, we must take action to protect Her integrity. Yes, relationships will suffer, but that was guaranteed when the sinful deed was accomplished. God promised that the wages of sin are death, and they are paid in full when someone willingly sins. There is grace, but not license.

Leaders must lead, and in this arena, lead quickly, strongly, and towards redemption and righteousness. If fraud is discovered, strong, Biblical leadership is critical.

How did "The Church Across Town" navigate these waters?

"The Church Across Town"

Earlier I told you that when I discovered the check with one signature, made out to Administrator Sam, we immediately and appropriately took him to lunch and confronted him. While that was a good start, it was not enough. Listen to what Sam was thinking in answering the following question:

Did you ever think about, or have a fear of getting caught?

Administrator Sam: Oh, sure. Yeah, I'm surprised it didn't happen sooner, really. I mean, I know when I look back on it, there were a couple times when you questioned some things. There was one time when you and Pastor and I sat down and there was some reconciliation about some things you had questions on.

Yes. So I felt like, that yes, that I was being found out. But maybe not to the extent that maybe I was. And I don't know if I realized to what extent, I know I didn't realize to what extent. That's the part that I've struggled with through all of this, is kind of figuring up and laying out an account of what had happened in that very beginning part to lead me down this path of deception.

It was sin that had taken over my thought process. But I knew what I was doing. It was difficult, but... No, it never really got easier.

I was a thief.

In our attempt to trust and believe the best, Pastor Bill and I let the first offense go, without adding additional constraints and/or increased verification. Hindsight is 20/20, but I sure wish we had asked more questions and handled this differently.

Action Questions

1. What keeps people from being willing to deal with fraud when they suspect it? Why?

2. As you think about the tension between extending grace to the fallen and demanding justice for their action, how does that fit into dealing with fraud in your mind?

3. Is your church prepared to deal with a discovery of fraud?

4. What goes through your mind when you read Sam's last statement in this chapter?

10 How to Clean Up After the Fire

*I think that the start was finally getting together
and sitting across the table from you, and then Pastor,
and being able to just articulate in a genuine way
how sorry I was that I messed up and broke that trust.*
~Sam

As we walk through the aftermath of the discovery and investigation of fraud, we then have to think about and walk through the cleanup process with care. Many lives are involved and we must remember that these are real people dealing with very real pain. How we proceed can determine whether the ministry survives or slowly dies.

A Case in Point – How Not to Handle

There was an emergency meeting called of the elder board of the church. The Senior Pastor was retiring and called for a financial audit to make sure he left his long-term ministry with a clean report. Prior to the arrival of an audit team, the longtime church administrator admitted to stealing $60,000 of church funds over the last year or two.

The board was shocked, hurting, literally crying as they described what happened. They were not trained for this nor were they prepared to deal with it. The board was sharply divided between a public hanging and the grace of restoration. The biggest problem the board had was that at least one person on the board kept leaking the content of the confidential meetings to key church members, and they in turn were spreading rumors, some true, many not true, about the theft and how leaders were handling or not handling the process. WOW!

With the rumor mill in full swing, the church was about to explode.

They asked us for our help, which we provided. I (Glenn) warned them up front that the fraud was likely five times as deep, five times as wide, and that they should be prepared to deal with that outcome.

They immediately said I was wrong because, "The administrator already confessed to $60,000 over an 18 month period and he paid it all back!" I told them it would be much worse, and they did not believe it!

Halfway into the investigation, when we got to 2.5 years and $180,000 dollars, they told us to stop. "Do not file a report. Take your staff and go home. We have seen and heard enough. Send us a bill."

A month later, as the rumors continued to flow from an unethical board member, the leadership asked me to come back and speak to entire congregation on a Sunday morning.

There are so many things wrong with this process that we don't have enough pages in a book to explain, but I think you get the idea. Suffice it to say, how we handle the cleanup really matters! If the Church is going to survive, we must get this part right.

The key to handling the cleanup properly is goal setting, planning, and then executing the plan. There are a wide variety of considerations and options, but the most important step is to decide upfront what your goal(s) is/are in the process, then the actions you take will make more sense.

Case in Point – A Story of Success

You remember earlier, when I, at age 29, was faced with confronting my boss about his seven years of stealing from the seminary? The first thing I did was partner with a trusted colleague and we set our goals. Before we took any action, we decided on what we wanted to accomplish.

1) First and foremost we wanted to put an end to the stealing.

2) We wanted the tens of thousands of dollars returned.

3) We wanted him to get the help he needed.

So we devised an action plan surrounding our goals. We confronted the man stealing and gave him 48 hours to meet with the President and confess. If he chose not to comply with our plan, we would be forced into another set of actions.

Fortunately for us, he met with the President and confessed. Most of the money was returned, and while we made a provision for him to get help, sadly, we are not sure he ever took advantage of the opportunity.

All in all, the end result turned out as good as it could have possibly been, given the circumstances. The culprit quit stealing and the majority of the money was returned. The institution's reputation was kept intact and long-term changes were made to help prevent future occurrences of fraud.

In addition to the tension between the "give them grace" and "they need to be hanged" people, there is a difficult line to walk between punishment and redemption. Depending on the degree of fraud, this line can become blurred with passion and deeply felt emotions.

Because of the sensitive and volatile nature of fraud, you will need a trusted leader with a calm, clear mind to lead through this process of cleanup. A good principle to follow is to involve as few people as possible, and only those who really need to be part of the process. Opinions will be flying and emotional strain will be high, so choose wisely.

Most governance forms require immediate board notification and board monitoring, but even if yours doesn't, the leadership needs to be involved. The board may or may not designate actions, depending on governance, and they may handle it or delegate it to someone else more qualified. Check your policies and procedures to see if there is a prescribed process in place, and follow as possible. If there is not a current policy in place, we would recommend establishing one as soon as possible. Thinking through these types of events in advance are always easier when not embroiled in one.

If there are staff serving in the ministry, consider how to break the news to them, for whatever is said will spread throughout the organization quickly. News travels fast, and this type flies.

Perhaps a meeting needs to be called to carefully explain the situation. Share as many details as you righteously can, but remember, what you share may come back upon you at a later time.

Staff members, both those paid and volunteers, will have suffered some measure of betrayal from their leader or co-worker's fraud. They may need to talk, receive counseling, or at least guidance on what to share and to whom. Remember, it will be difficult to over communicate with those who are hurt.

Do not be afraid to get outside help. Although there is a cost to this, there is a much greater cost of mishandling a delicate process like this.

Beyond dealing with the board, staff, volunteers, and the membership, there is the public to consider. How the news breaks and the extent of the fraud will help determine what needs to be shared publically and when.

If a story breaks on the front page of the local paper, a response team needs to be ready, whereas if the fraud does not reach the public's eye, then perhaps a much lower response is in order.

Governance will dictate some of this area, but don't underestimate the value of good judgment. There are equally good arguments for keeping things *undisclosed* versus *full disclosure.*

Considerations include:

- How will public knowledge help or hurt those involved?
- How will the congregation be impacted?
- How will the community be impacted?
- How will the Kingdom of God be impacted?
- How will the individual and their family members be impacted?
- How many different ways will this story end up being spun and what are the possible damages with partial truth being shared?

No one sins in a vacuum and fraud is a sin. The person's family will be impacted in negative ways. We have a responsibility to be as gentle as we can be in dealing with this sin. The spouse, children, extended family, and their friends will all be affected, and what we say, or not, will either help or hinder healing and redemption.

Doing unto others how we would like to be treated should be considered. Yes, the person violated our trust, but their family most likely did not. We need to tread this water carefully and consider the wise words of the Apostle Paul:

> Brothers, if anyone is caught in any transgression, you who are spiritual should restore him in a spirit of gentleness. Keep watch on yourself, lest you too be tempted. Bear one another's burdens, and so fulfill the law of Christ.
>
> Galatians 6:1-2 (ESV)

We must seek to walk in a "spirit of gentleness" and to help "bear one another's burdens" through this difficult time.

Prayerfully consider what is shared and how. Is a written announcement read publically the best way? Should this information be presented during a normal service or gathering, or perhaps during a special meeting? Should the guilty person be involved or even part of the meeting?

Other issues to consider are redemption, restitution, and continuing in the relationship. Of course, many of these will be determined by the action that caused the problem in the first place. An unrepentant thief caught will probably be dealt with differently than someone who freely confesses and seeks to redeem the situation.

What is necessary for redemption to occur?

- Admission?
- Acceptance of responsibility?
- Disclosure?
- Apology?
- Restitution?

- Penitence?
- Punishment?

These are all very difficult questions to sort through, especially under the pressure of a fraud case. Trust takes time to rebuild and once it is destroyed, it is very difficult to reacquire.

There are those who are very familiar with how to handle dealing with the devastation caused by fraud, so we would strongly recommend that you consider hiring outside assistance.

Follow up and closures with the people involved in fraud are a very important part of redemption, as well as closure for them and the ministry. The person who committed the fraud needs to understand his new relationship with the ministry. This may range from no relationship to some sort of probation to complete restoration, depending on the circumstances. Communication is critical so there are no misunderstandings.

In addition, there have been times when someone has been a "serial fraud perpetrator" and it is imperative that follow-up is included in your action plan. Establish processes for follow-up for the individual to ensure that other ministries are not impacted by this same character flaw if the person moves on from your ministry.

If you are unwilling to appropriately deal with this aspect, the person may move on to another ministry and commit fraud, sometimes with multiple ministries. While this kind of follow-up is at times difficult, we must put the Kingdom first to protect other ministries, as well as the individual, from repetition of this sinful behavior.

If handled properly, the discovery of and properly dealing with fraud can be redemptive for the ministry. Our God specializes in turning messy, difficult situations into growth opportunities for the Kingdom.

"The Church Across Town"

Pastor Bill: You know, the problem is that if this person finds themselves and they are reading the book today, you're in deep - you've done this for years, and you think you've taken more than you could every pay back. And you think, 'I can never pay this back;' you're thinking $100,000, "how am I ever going to un-do this?' Well, I think it goes back to a similar type response. It's just harder. I think that person needs to find someone to tell. And it can be very, very, very difficult to tell a mate, or to tell a close friend, or maybe their supervisor, but I think getting that out on the table is the only place they are going to get rescued from it.

Repentance begins with acceptance of the fact that we have violated God's will and His clearly revealed standards. If we are walking in the wrong direction, away from God and His word, we must stop, turn around, and walk in the opposite direction if we ever hope to change. Sinful behavior began with a decision and so does repentance.

Treasurer Cindy: But we took a biblical approach to it, straight out of the Bible, and I think without that foresight, that guidance, of knowing what the Bible says to do in that situation really would've got us off track. So I was happy how it played out and the agreements that were made.

Conflict is not a stranger to those in church leadership. When sin is discovered, the Scriptures must be our standard of how to deal with it. Achieving the balance between grace and punitive actions might very well determine the survival of the ministry.

Administrator Sam: No, you still, if you don't come forward, you're still going to be found out at some point in time and the consequences are not good. I'm not saying that I would've been able to continue in my position at the church, which I shouldn't be, but there may have still been some ways for me to continue being a part of that community of believers, especially with the staff, and you know, it just isn't worth it - with the grace of God. And if there's work between the group, there is a way for restitution to happen, whether that be, of course, financially, but part of it is just the reconciliation with that group of people that you have confidence in. That's worth more than any amount of money.

"Your sin will find you out," is an old saying and also true. The deeds done in darkness will be shouted from the rooftop. By God's good grace, wise leadership, and outside counsel, the church in our book not only survived this drama, but continues on today.

There is pain, family strains, and relationships broken that would be restored this side of heaven, but we rest in knowing our God is redemptive – even in cases of fraud.

"The Church Across Town" was able to work through the betrayal and trust violations and restoration was gained through restitution and repentance. Sadly, many of these type situations do not work out so well.

Navigating through the smoke of fraud is often painful and difficult. We do rest in the fact that our God is redemptive and also uses even our worst failures to bring about good in our lives. Most of us are familiar with Romans 8:28:

And we know that for those who love God all things work together for good, for those who are called according to his purpose. (ESV)

Perhaps quoting verse 27 would be helpful as well:

And he who searches hearts knows what is the mind of the Spirit, because the Spirit intercedes for the saints according to the will of God. (ESV)

The Spirit is interceding for the saints and in the case of church fraud; we can also rest in this truth. Seeking the Lord's favor, grace, and wisdom is paramount in cases like these, for the potential for destruction is great. However, so is the potential for revival! If handled properly, growth in obedience, holiness, and general fear of the Lord can have a cleansing effect on a local body of believers.

Our God specializes in building beautiful trophies from the ashes of sinful choices, if we will but yield to His hand and ways. Yes, fire causes great damage, but it also can purify and pave the way to new life if we will let it.

Action Questions:

1. Where would you land on the spectrum between "give them grace," and "hang them?" Why?

2. After reading this book, think about the last public fraud scandal you heard about. What could they have done to prevent it? Did they handle the public aspects of it well or poorly? Explain.

3. What is the difference between restoration and repentance? Between forgiveness and a restored relationship? Between punishment and restitution?

4. Which would you and your ministry like to spend its resources and time on, fraud cleanup or fraud prevention?

11 Lessons Learned from "The Church Across Town"

Oh, just the friendships that have been lost and...that's really it. When it comes to just the personal...I mean we've been, my wife and I have been in that church for 30 plus years and then to walk away, which I think was the right thing to do. And I'm...but that's what hurt. Most of our friends are already gone anywhere from there, but yet...yeah, just that. You know, and I'm disappointed in myself. ~Sam

This chapter contains some of the remaining excerpts from the three interviewees, Pastor Bill, Treasurer Cindy, and Church Administer Sam, the fraudster. Our hope is that God will use their testimonies to touch those currently committing fraud and help them turn from their sinful ways, and/or hopefully prevent fraud before it happens for all the rest of us.

Q: What is your greatest regret in all of this?

Administrator Sam: That I lied to my pastor, my colleagues, and my friends, and I will never likely regain their trust. And that I deeply hurt my wife and my family in all of this.

Q: Pastor Bill, what did you see as the greatest loss in all of this?

Pastor Bill: The loss of a friend, and a long time church family. As his pastor I wish I could have seen it sooner, I wish I could have helped prevent it.

Q: Treasurer Cindy, looking back, what disturbs you the most about all of this?

Treasurer Cindy: The betrayal of a trusted friend. Oh, I was sick to my stomach. Just literally sick to my stomach. Not feeling...losing appetite. I was tired at the end of those meetings. It shook me to the core. Biggest regret is I didn't see it sooner. Biggest regret, I felt like maybe I slept on the job, a little bit. I mean, I probably should have caught it sooner...

Finally, each of the participants of this tragic drama that plunged "The Church Across Town" into such a mess was asked to share any observations or recommendations. Please prayerfully consider their thoughts.

Pastor Bill: It's crazy that church members expect you to be everywhere all the time. And, you know, because of that I think as a staff people, we begin to look at ways to compensate ourselves, to make up for that. And I wonder if a lot of the feelings begins there, because, you know, I had to do x, y, and z and I think the church sometimes doesn't mind taking advantage of staff people. And so the staff people don't mind taking advantage of the church. We need to take better care of our staff, physically, emotionally, and spiritually.

I remember thinking to myself during the denial stage, there is definitely the feeling of "It cannot be". There must be a mistake. There must be an explanation. This cannot be as bad as it could be. And it is hard to nail down some of these things. You do have all the smoke and you don't see the flames, and you think, it just can't be that bad. Don't walk away from it, run toward the problem. Don't stick your head in the sand.

And I would just say that as a policy, it would be a good idea for the treasurer, the CFO, if those are two different people - which they probably should be – and the Pastor, should look through the financial statements and learn about what we spent money on. And then make sure it's going where we would like for it to go. You don't have to be an accountant to read a check register!

Know this for sure; your integrity will be tested. Be prepared. When your integrity is tested, it may end up costing you, but don't give, God will not be mocked.

Administrator Sam: First and foremost, you have to have accountability. And whether that comes from one individual or whether that be the Pastor or the financial individual on the committee or maybe or treasurer or something...but be accountable.

Second, try to find creative ways to regularly appreciate your staff. It doesn't have to be money, and it doesn't necessarily mean parading them up in front of the congregation and slapping them on the back, but find creative ways to show appreciation that are meaningful to them.

Treasurer Cindy: Build strong accountabilities and stick with them. Make sure you have in place good policies and procedures. Verify! I don't want you to have to go through what our church did. Satan, it's his world, he will be defeated on the other side. But until then, it's a war. You've got to do your best to prevent it.

Final Thoughts from the Authors

Glenn: I have worked nearly 40 cases of fraud in the church. I have seen firsthand the devastation, the bewilderment, and the utter chaos that ensues.

Relationships broken forever, leadership that will never be trusted again, churches destroyed, and the worst thing of all, those who will leave the church because of the hypocrisy and negligence of Her leaders, and those who will never come to Christ because of our collective bad example. It is the cry of my heart that God and His Holy Spirit will overwhelm you and your church and call you to take the necessary steps to thwart the enemy's efforts to discredit and destroy His church. May his Kingdom come, on earth as it is in heaven.

Rod: When asked, "Why are there criminals in the church?", the answer is really quite simple. Because they are in the world. The Fall distorted all of creation, a fact not withheld by God in His word. Cain took his brother's life. Achan pocketed what his eyes coveted. David took Uriah's wife. Judas betrayed Jesus. Ananias and Sapphira misrepresented their gift. The list of bad behaving people in the bible is extensive.

Therefore, the church is exhorted to put on the full armor of God in order to "stand firm against the schemes of the Devil" (Ephesians 6:10-12, NASB). In John 10:10, we are reminded the thief comes to "steal and kill and destroy." Jesus, in speaking of His promised return, uses theft prevention to illustrate his point.

> But be sure of this, that if the head of the house had known at what time of the night the thief was coming, he would have been on the alert and would not have allowed his house to be broken into. For this reason you also must be ready...
>
> Matthew 24:43-44 (NASB)

It is our hope and prayer this resource helps you and your church be ready and alert.

Jeff: Jesus said He would build His Church and for that I am very grateful. Until that task is completed, we must continue working and seeking to excel in integrity and faithfulness.

We have a passion for this topic because we have walked through the unbelievable pain associated with fraud. Until you have looked into the eyes of someone devastated by this crime, it is hard to grasp the severity of, and pain inflicted by, it.

Families are destroyed, marriages break up, young people reject Christ, and many sheep are slaughtered due to fraud. Sexual fraud or financial fraud, the results are the same. Sooner or later the sin will be uncovered and someone, probably several people, will be entrusted with trying to bring answers to the inevitable questions – How could this happen? What do we do now? Who is to blame? At some point the pain settles down into numbness and other questions arise – Where do we get help? How do we go on? What is going to happen to us? What do we do about...? Can we keep it from happening again?

My desire is that every pastor, elder, and leader would read these pages and take whatever steps are necessary to never have to walk through what we all have had to on far too many occasions.

We trust and hope that what was shared in this book will assist you in raising the level of integrity in your ministry. We are ambassadors for Christ and citizens of His Kingdom. How we conduct our business in this world reflects upon Him and His Church, and we pray we would rise to this challenge.

One driving question we raise is,

Why can't the Church of Jesus Christ be the leader in integrity?

Shouldn't She be?

Appendix

We trust the information provided so far has been beneficial. In this last section we have included some articles and resources that will further your work in becoming the best steward possible over the ministry God has entrusted to your care.

First, we have included a variety of articles that deal with scammers, peddlers, and fraud areas you may not have considered. These are followed by our self-evaluation checklist to help you determine the areas that need work in your ministry. Finally, we have included many helpful forms and sample policies for your consideration. Please feel free to use any or all of them to enhance your anti-fraud efforts.

Articles
"When the Church Profits from Fraud"
"Affinity Fraud: The Silent Disgrace"
"When Fraud Comes Knocking"
"5 Fraud Tips Every Business Leader Should Act On"
"Why not Lead with Integrity?"
"Typical Financial Statement Services from Accountants/CPAs"

Anti-Fraud Ministry Checklist

Sample Forms/Policies
Offering Counting Agreement Forms
Crisis Communication Teams Policy
Whistle-Blower
Credit Card
Anti-Fraud
Record Retention

When the Church Profits from Fraud
Dr. Rodney Harrison

A friend and associate of ours (Glenn and Rod) was known for his generosity to the church staff and others. In many cases, this involved providing iPads and similar devices to pastors and select members. However, an FBI investigation revealed the generosity was funded by the theft of these items at his previous place of employment.

According to Frank Sommerville, an attorney and CPA with Church Law & Tax, "if one steals property or money the ownership does not change. The thief cannot give away something he does not own." The implications for the church are that if through criminal activity someone gives the church stolen property or money, the ownership remains with the original owner, not the church. Therefore, the church is obligated to give it to the rightful owner.

In a highly publicized case in Kansas City, a pharmacist diluted chemo drugs and sold them as full-strength. According to his testimony, he began selling the diluted drugs to fulfill a $1,000,000 pledge to his church.[3] A decade later, the crime was discovered, and the church, at great financial sacrifice, gave hundreds of thousands to support cancer victims.

If the church profits from the fraudulent activities of members, what legal and moral obligations do you have? In many cases, the legal answers are not black and white.

This year (2015) an NBC affiliate in Michigan reported on a church's decision not to give back funds donated by a

---

[3] http://www.cbsnews.com/news/thousands-of-diluted-drug-doses/ accessed April 30, 2015.

convicted felon. In this case, the United States Attorney General's office had asked the church to reimburse $300,000 of donations. In a statement released to the media, the Attorney General stated, "The United States Attorney's Office must try and return assets stolen from innocent investors as restitution. We requested that various third parties (including the church) voluntarily reimburse or return funds received..." It took the church several months to come to this decision, and the outcome has been a firestorm of publicity in the court of public opinion. Even if the church is not legally required to return contributions, it is wise to have written policy or agreement in place if such an event arises.

Leaders should take into consideration the complexities of the issues, which include:

- How will the decision align with the vision of the church?
- Can a determination be made to the amount received through criminal actions verses gifts from legal activities?
- Has the money been spent?
- Did anyone in leadership know, or have cause to believe, the contributions were acquired from criminal actions?
- Can a case for rightful ownership be made?
- Is the church and leadership comfortable with possible legal actions against the church?

As a church planter in California, the question came up, "Does your church accept tithes from illegal workers?" Up until that time, I had never given the source of contributions a thought. In a well-publicized case in 2008, a Florida pastor against the expansion of gaming refused a $600,000 gift from a lottery winner. The decision was lauded by some and laughed at by others. Seven years later, the church is doing fine; the pastor is still at the church. It seems his integrity has been rewarded.

Affinity Fraud: The Silent Disgrace
Dr. Rodney Harrison

Affinity fraud refers to investment or financial scams that prey upon the members of affinity groups, such as religious or ethnic communities, the elderly or professional groups. In the church, these scams net billions of dollars each year. Many victims never come forward due to ignorance or shame. The criminals committing these fraudulent scams are often members or regular attendees. Often, the scammer enlists the pastor or other respected leader in the church, who unwittingly enlists others.

Many affinity scams are pyramid or Ponzi schemes. The perpetrator will usually be a new member or attendee, whose job is related to financial management, an investment company or a start-up company. This new member will establish good will through generous gifts, nice dinners and a lavish lifestyle, which are attributed to the "blessings of God" and "wise investments."

Once the scammer has laid the foundation of trust, he will "donate" a gift of stock or similar gifts to the pastor. Over the next few months, "dividend" checks or interest payments start arriving. For example, if the "gift" was supposedly 100 shares of stock worth $5000, a quarterly check might arrive for $750. The next quarter, another check arrives for $1,150. The investment is paying off, and the scammer mentions that the company is expanding. Thoroughly duped, the pastor invests $10,000, and three months later, receives checks for $1,300 in addition to another payment from the original "investment."

With visions of double-digit returns of their investments, the pastor or leaders are interested in how to invest more. The scammer will insist that this is limited investment opportunity, and is sorry he cannot allow more people to invest. Then, out of the blue (about the time another check arrives), the doors open for additional investments, but only large ones, as the company is expanding. The pastor is now in recruiting mode, and tells members about this great opportunity. The members he invites are usually those near retirement (thus sizable retirement accounts) or those with high net worth. Of course, the key to the scam is the pastor's "testimony" of how wonderful this investment has been to him and his family. This "special group" of investors allows the scammer to "move" retirement funds to the new investment, and is assured the investment is sound, legal and safe. Once members have invested hundreds of thousands, if not millions of retirement dollars into the scam, the "dividend" checks dry up, and the scammer leaves town.

In the case above, the total "dividends" paid out by the scammer before the first dollars changed hands was only $1,900, plus the cost of some dinners and generous gifts to the church. The scam could easily be funded by $5,000 or less. After the first "investment" of $10,000 by the pastor, a few more dividend checks are sent to the pastor, but the scammer already has made a net profit. This is not the goal, however, and these scams often result in losses into the millions from a single congregation. Sadly, most affinity fraud goes unprosecuted. The scammer may use an alias and employ elaborate schemes to cover the crime.

To protect your church from affinity fraud, the U.S. Securities and Exchange Commission recommends the following guidelines for all investments:

Check out everything - no matter how trustworthy the person seems who brings the investment opportunity to your attention. Never make an investment based solely on the recommendation of a member of an organization or religious or ethnic group to which you belong. Investigate the investment thoroughly and check the truth of every statement you are told about the investment. Be aware that the person telling you about the investment may have been fooled into believing that the investment is legitimate when it is not.

Do not fall for investments that promise spectacular profits or "guaranteed" returns. If an investment seems too good to be true, then it probably is. Similarly, be extremely leery of any investment that is said to have no risks; very few investments are risk-free. The greater the potential return from an investment, the greater your risk of losing money. Promises of fast and high profits, with little or no risk, are classic warning signs of fraud.

Be skeptical of any investment opportunity that is not in writing. Fraudsters often avoid putting things in writing, but legitimate investments are usually in writing. Avoid an investment if you are told they do "not have the time to reduce to writing" the particulars about the investment. You should also be suspicious if you are told to keep the investment opportunity confidential.

Don't be pressured or rushed into buying an investment before you have a chance to think about - or investigate - the "opportunity." Just because someone you know made money, or claims to have made money, doesn't mean you will, too. Be especially skeptical of investments that are pitched as "once-in-a-lifetime" opportunities, particularly when the promoter bases the recommendation on "inside" or confidential information.

Another type of affinity fraud can involve unsolicited gifts. Below is an actual email (with names changed) that cost a local church over $40,000, which was every dollar they had in savings and checking.

Dear Pastor,

Recently my Doctor told me that I would not last for the next eight months due to cancer. Having known my condition I have decided to donate my estate to a church that will utilize this money propagating the word of God and to endeavor that the house of God is maintained. The Bible made us to understand that blessed is the hand that giveth.

I don't want a situation where this money will be used in an ungodly way. This is why I am taking this decision. I am not afraid of death hence I know where I am going. I know that I am going to be in the bosom of the Lord. Exodus 14:14

As soon as I receive your reply I shall give you the contact information for my bank here in Wichita. I will also issue you an authority letter that will establish your church as beneficiary of this fund. I want you and the church to pray for me

during my illness, but in joy, because the Lord is my shepherd.
　Sincerely,
　Mercy Hardin

In this scam, the bank information was actually a scammer's computer. When bank transfer information was shared, the scammer was able to access the church's checking and savings accounts, withdrawing all but $1 from each account.

Affinity fraud costs churches $50,000,000,000 per year.[4] That is $170 for every person in America, each year, every year. With numbers like that, pastors need to take the dangers of affinity fraud in the church seriously.

---

[4] The Economist, January 28, 2012.
http://www.economist.com/node/21543526, accessed May 9, 2015.

When Fraud Comes Knocking
Dr. Rodney Harrison

It will be only a matter of time before someone comes asking for assistance with gas, food, utilities or cash. Often, the person dealing with this request is the least equipped to respond to such situations, such as receptionists, secretaries or volunteers. A typical outcome is to fork over $20 in the hope that the "visitor" leaves, or to call the pastor to deal with the request.

As Christians, we want to do the right thing at all times. Ironically, panhandlers and scammers know that, and prey upon churches that are unprepared when fraud comes knocking.

Almost every time I teach about this fraud in the form of con artists and scammers, someone brings up Matthew 25:35-40. Let's look at this passage together:

> 'For I was hungry and you gave Me something to eat; I was thirsty and you gave Me something to drink; I was a stranger and you took Me in; I was naked and you clothed Me; I was sick and you took care of Me; I was in prison and you visited Me.'
>
> "Then the righteous will answer Him, 'Lord, when did we see You hungry and feed You, or thirsty and give You something to drink? When did we see You a stranger and take You in, or without clothes and clothe You? When did we see You sick, or in prison, and visit You?'

> "And the King will answer them, 'I assure
> you: Whatever you did for one of the least of
> these brothers of Mine, you did for Me.'"

Notice that the King indicates, "Whatever you did for
one of the least of these brothers of Mine, you did for Me."
It can be argued that Jesus is speaking of "the
brotherhood of man" and the passage applies to anyone
who is hungry, thirsty, in need of lodging or cloth.
Ironically, most members who accept this interpretation
expect the church to respond with appropriate
benevolence, while they personally never would invite
these folks into their homes.

The King in this text is the One who separates the
sheep from the goats (v. 32). The best understanding of
the phrase translated "brothers of Mine" are the followers
of Jesus. As believers, we are responsible to demonstrate
brotherly love. This is consistent with Paul's words in
Galatians 6:10, "So then, as we have opportunity, let us
do good to everyone, and especially to those who are of the
household of faith." Earlier in Galatians 6, we are
reminded, "Do not be deceived." With that exhortation,
consider ways of responding to those who come knocking.

Dealing with Con Artists

Con artists and scammers will try to make you feel
guilty for not helping them. The result is often a $20 bill.
Con artists are essentially saying, "I am a ministry
opportunity. Take me on...NOW."

In the church, new ministries should be at God's
invitation, should honor God and support the purpose,

ministry and mission of the church. When one thinks about it, giving a con artist money to buy a bottle of booze does not meet even one of the above stipulations.

By definition, a con artist is one who conceals, falsifies, and deceives people who could assist them. The key words are *conceal, falsify,* and *deceive.* In scripture, believers are exhorted to be on guard for those who would practice such things.

- Behold, I send you out as sheep in the midst of wolves. Therefore be wise as serpents and harmless as doves. (Matthew 10:16)
- Be sober, be vigilant; because your adversary the devil walks about like a roaring lion, seeking whom he may devour. (1 Peter 5:8)
- For what fellowship has righteousness with lawlessness? And what communion has light with darkness? (2 Corinthians 6:14)
- For you were once darkness, but now you are light in the Lord. Walk as children of the light ... And have no fellowship with the unfruitful works of darkness, but rather expose them. (Ephesians 5:8)

A young mother comes into the office. "Can you help us? Me and my husband ran out of gas, and don't have no money to buy gas because our car needed fixin'. We're on our way to Texas, where Joe, my husband, has a job waiting. We spent our last $20 on formula for the baby. If you could spare a twenty, we could get to (the next town) where we've got some family.

Her voice drops a bit. 'It's just a loan. We'll mail it right back to you, soon as we get our first paycheck."

At this point you see a young man standing by an older car, clutching a blanket-swaddled bundle you assume is the couple's infant. Your kind heart says to give this young woman the $20 she asks for. But your common sense says otherwise. So which do you listen to?

If you're like many, you'll reach into your pocket and fork over the twenty. You've likely just been a victim of one of many distressed stranger scams. It is not unusual for teams to make $200 or more per day using this scam.

Another scam that comes knocking is the "service personnel" who comes by unexpectedly to service your computers, copier, phone, furnace or air-conditioning. These scammers will often drive up in a service van and are wearing official looking uniforms. After securing information about the system they are "servicing" they leave. A week later the church will receive an invoice for services, payable to a P.O. box or out of state address. Such scams often go undetected, and can net the scammers thousands of dollars in a matter of weeks.

What to Do When Dealing with Solicitations

1. Never be unkind to any person. Treat them with the same respect as you would want to be treated if you were in need. Nevertheless, understand that if you turn someone down or attempt to verify the need, they may not respond appropriately to your kindness, no matter how well treated.
2. Get your church to set policies and procedures for benevolence and solicitations, and follow the policy.
3. Keep a log of persons and their requests.

4. Develop and keep an up-to-date list of avenues of assistance. Know the service agencies within your city.
5. Remember, gas cards or grocery certificates are not a solution. These are often sold for cash or used for the purpose given, but not because the person needed food or gas.
6. Set up policies on ordering supplies. Know your sales people. Call to verify anyone who comes by unexpectedly to service computers, phones, internet connections, heating air-conditioners and similar service calls.
7. Share the gospel. Try to find out the person's relationship with Jesus. This may be a providential encounter!

As noted earlier, secretaries and volunteers are often the least trained to deal with con artists, and yet are the ones who answer the "knock on the door." If this describes your church, here are some ideas to help on the front lines.

1. Invite local law enforcement or other scam experts to share insights on dealing with con artists.
2. Have a written plan for assistance and supplies. Since the safety of staff and volunteers is the foremost concern, ensure the policy does not put people in danger. It is better to reimburse $20 than put someone at risk.
3. Be alert; if something seems strange, take time to check it out.

4. Over time, it is likely some will "use" or "abuse" your church's benevolence. However, if you have helped in sincerity, and with the goal of being redemptive, it is better to err on the side of compassion instead of being uncompassionate.

At one church I (Rod) pastored, requests for benevolence were weekly occurrences. This was despite the fact the church was small and rural. Almost immediately I discovered the church gave "gas cards" to anyone who came by asking for money. Soon, word got out that the church was "open for business." After a month, a benevolence policy was put into place. The next Sunday, like clockwork, a truck pulled up. The occupants needed gas money to get to Jefferson City, about 100 miles away. As I greeted our "guests," I mentioned that the church had a new benevolence policy. It would only take a few minutes, and I reminded them that the church had a benevolence limit of a 10 gallon gas card. But first, I had a form to fill out before I could make a benevolence decision. The questions are printed on this form:

Benevolence Request Form
1. Date and Time:

2. Requestors Name:

3. Address

4. Cell Phone/Email

5. Vehicle: (license, type make, model, color)

6. Is this your first time requesting assistance? [ ] Yes   [ ] No

7. Type of request

Please write a short description of the person(s) requesting assistance on the back:
Approximate Height
Approximate Weight
Hair Color
Other Distinguishing Marks
Was the person alone or with others
Result of call to local law enforcement
(555) 555-1212

Note the final step is to call the non-emergency number of the local law-enforcement. This could be the police, sheriff or highway patrol. In this church, the call went to the local sheriff office that was aware of our benevolence policy. Ironically, the conversation usually went like this,

> "Hello, this is____ from Friendship church. I have a couple seeking gas money. The requestor is John Doe from Any Town, driving a late model Ford pickup with Kansas plates." The operator would then ask, "Is this an emergency," to which I would answer, "No, we are just reporting this information in case
> these might be persons of interest. Thank you for your time."

The first time the policy was put into place, as soon as the call was placed, our guests left, grumbling "this church don't trust nobody." That was the last time anyone came seeking gas money, as the con artist network soon knew the gas station was closed!

There is no end to the scams con artists attempt. Here are a few that I have personally encountered:

- Asphalt Paving/Driveway Sealing Scam. The church is approached through door-to-door solicitation by suspects indicating that they have been working in the neighborhood and they noticed that the victim's driveway needed repair work. They have extra material, and can do the job at a great price.
- The prescription scam. They need money to fill a medical prescription. These scammers always have

a copy of the pill bottle and prescription, and will get a refund as soon as you leave.

- The car broke down, and I have no money left. These scammers will pick up auto-parts receipts to "prove" they had an unexpected expense.
- Going to a funeral, and lost their wallet or were robbed, and need money to make it to the funeral. These scammers will almost always have a copy of the death notice.

Con artists are those who want to fleece the sheep. The pastor is tasked with protecting the sheep. The time invested in helping the church develop policies and training for staff and volunteers is time well spent.

5 Fraud Tips Every Business Leader Should Act On

Association of Certified Fraud Examiners, Inc.

Organizations around the world lose an estimated 5 percent of their annual revenues to fraud, according to the ACFE's 2014 *Report to the Nations on Occupational Fraud and Abuse.* A single instance of fraud can be devastating: the median loss per fraud case in the ACFE study was $145,000, and more than a fifth of the cases involved losses of at least $1 million. The good news? There are some basic steps your organization can take immediately to lessen your vulnerability to fraud:

Be Proactive

Adopt a code of ethics for management and employees. Evaluate your internal controls for effectiveness and identify areas of the business that are vulnerable to fraud.

Establish Hiring Procedures

When hiring staff, conduct thorough background investigations. Check educational, credit and employment history (as permitted by law), as well as references.

Train Employees in Fraud Prevention

Do workers know the warning signs of fraud? Ensure that staff members know basic fraud prevention techniques.

Implement a Fraud Hotline

Fraud is still most likely to be detected by a tip. Providing an anonymous reporting system for your employees, contractors and clients will help uncover more fraud.

Increase the Perception of Detection

Communicate regularly to staff about anti-fraud policies, ways to report suspicions of misconduct, and the potential consequences (including termination and prosecution) of fraudulent behavior.
Implementing these tips could help prevent your organization from becoming a statistic – so take action today.

Designing an Effective Anti-Fraud Training Program

Who Should Attend?

Every employee within the organization should be mandated to participate in the fraud awareness training program. No individuals — regardless of their position within the organization — should be provided an exemption from receiving an initial orientation and ongoing anti-fraud education.

Training for Managers and Executives

In addition to the information presented to all employees, managers and executives should receive special training that addresses the added fraud prevention and detection responsibility — and ability — provided by their positions of authority. For example, department managers should be trained in the specific warning signs and prevention/detection methods pertinent to their department's functions. Purchasing managers should be well versed in the red flags of bribery schemes; likewise, controllers should understand just how important their vigilance is in preventing and detecting fraudulent disbursements.

Frequency and Length of Fraud Awareness Training

Like any educational efforts, frequent exposure to anti-fraud topics is the key to ensuring employees absorb — and apply — the information provided. Formal fraud awareness training should be an ongoing process that begins at the time of hire. Employees should also participate in refresher training at least annually to help keep the program alive and engrained in their minds. Additionally, all employees should sign an annual statement acknowledging their understanding of and commitment to the program.

Training Delivery Methods

Formal anti-fraud training can take many forms, including live, in-class instruction; recorded video or animated courses; or interactive self-study programs. Of these options, a live class is preferable, as it allows employees the opportunity to actively participate, interact with other employees, discuss the true fraud risks facing the organization, and seek and provide feedback regarding the anti-fraud program as a whole. Integrating games and role-playing exercises into the training curriculum can make the course more enjoyable — and thus more effective — for participants. Everyone involved in the ministry should be mandated to participate in the fraud awareness training program. No individuals — regardless of their position within the organization — should be provided an exemption from receiving an initial orientation and ongoing anti-fraud education.

Targeted Training for Managers and Executives

Perhaps most important, however, is that the training be based on the realities of the organization, rather than on generic anti-fraud messages. While providing general information is good and necessary, doing so without addressing the specific concerns of the company or providing employees with practical knowledge and ideas on how to apply it will render the training program ineffective. In addition, the organization can use other informal means to reinforce its anti-fraud stance on a more constant basis. Periodic newsletters, posters in break rooms, and other casual reminders help keep fraud prevention and detection in the front of employees' minds.

Topics to Cover

The following topics should form the basis of the training, but the information presented should focus on the specific risks faced by the organization in order to provide employees with practical, implementable knowledge.

What Fraud Is and What It Is Not

A good anti-fraud training program informs employees of what behavior is acceptable and what is not. Providing employees with the legal definition of fraud is not enough; effective training includes an interactive discussion and examples of fraud, as well as examples of errors and abuse.

How Fraud Hurts the Organization

Surprisingly, some employees view the theft of a few thousand dollars from a big organization as having a negligible impact on the company as a whole. Others might believe that fudging numbers in the accounting records to enable the company to reach its goals is actually a helpful act. Fraud awareness training programs must make clear to employees how such actions harm the organization — how all frauds result in lost resources; decreased productivity; lowered morale; investments of time and money into investigation, punishment, and remediation; and a hit to the company's reputation.

How Fraud Hurts Employees

Employees must also be made aware of how a fraud perpetrated by another individual can negatively affect them personally through decreased salaries, loss of bonuses, possible layoffs, increased scrutiny, decreased trust throughout the organization, and the need to clean up after any mess created. Personalizing the fallout in this way helps increase employees' commitment to aiding fraud prevention and detection efforts.

Who Perpetrates Fraud

The fraud-triangle theory indicates that anyone who has the combination of sufficient pressure, adequate opportunity, and an ability to rationalize a dishonest act is at risk of committing fraud. Fraudsters come in all age groups, income levels, and from both genders. Further, ACFE research shows that the typical fraudster is college educated and does not have a criminal history. Anti-fraud training should work to dispel any preconceived notions held by employees regarding what a fraud perpetrator looks like, and help employees learn to focus on identifying the warning signs of fraudulent behavior.

How to Identify Fraud

Instructing employees that they must help the organization fight fraud does little good without some accompanying information about what to look for. The following are some warning signs of fraud that employees should be aware of:

Financial/Transactional Red Flags

- Red flags regarding the structure of or personnel involved in a transaction
- Red flags within the organization's operations
- Red flags within the accounting system
- Red flags regarding the organization's financial performance

Behavioral Red Flags

- Living beyond their means
- Financial difficulties
- Control issues, unwilling to share duties
- Unusually close relationship with vendor/customer
- Wheeler/dealer attitude
- Divorce/family problems

- Irritability, suspiciousness, defensiveness
- Addiction problems
- Unwilling to take vacation days
- Past employment-related problems
- Complained about inadequate pay
- Excessive pressure from within the organization
- Past legal problems
- Instability in life circumstances
- Excessive family/peer pressure for success
- Complained about lack of authority

How to Report Fraud

More fraud is uncovered by tips than by any other means, making employees the best possible fraud detection control. But for employees to be able to serve this function, they must be well informed on how to report any suspicious activity, as well as empowered to make such reports without risk of retribution.

The Punishment for Dishonest Acts

The opportunity to commit fraud becomes more attractive when employees believe fraud normally goes undetected and unprosecuted. Consequently, the punishment (termination and possible prosecution) should be spelled out explicitly to all employees in advance. Providing examples of past transgressions that have been punished can reinforce the stance that such acts will be addressed with certainty, swiftness, and severity.

©2012 Association of Certified Fraud Examiners, Inc.

Why Not Lead With Integrity?
Dr. Jeff Klick

It is interesting that God called His people, better stated, commanded His people, to be holy. Holy is a word that can be defined as "different" or "set apart." In both the Old and New Testament, the command is clear.

> For I am the Lord your God. Consecrate
> yourselves therefore, and be holy, for I am holy.
> Leviticus 11:44 (ESV)

> But as He who called you is holy, you also
> be holy in all your conduct, ...
> 1 Peter 1:15 (ESV)

If a man on the street survey was taken, I doubt holiness would be the top response to this question:

When you think of a Christian leader, what is the first word that comes into your mind?

While discouraging, it is even more so when we consider the public black eye received when a church leader steals or commits some other form of fraud. The news outlets seem to love freely sharing the sins of the Christian. When a well-known Christian is exposed as a cheat, thief, immoral or unfair in their dealings, the news receives above the fold exposure.

The Institute of Church Management was created by a good friend of mine. Glenn Miller saw a need for the Church and Christian ministry arena to step up in their financial integrity. Glenn often asks those attending the workshops offered by the Institute the following question:

Is there any reason why the Church cannot, or should not be, the financial integrity leaders in our communities?

The truth is that we all are an example to those around us. Will our behavior be a benchmark or an excuse? When we fail to lead in financial integrity, we provide an excuse for those that do not know Christ. Every time a Christian leader is caught in fraud, the Church suffers shame. Why can't the other side be true? If we would learn to lead with exemplary integrity, our light would shine brighter in the darkness.

The good news is that we can limit the potential damage of fraud through our procedures, and by gaining the appropriate knowledge. The Church does not need to continue down the same old path of failure. There is a movement beginning to change the way the Church does business. At least there should be. If there isn't one yet, then let's you and I begin one today.

The Church of Jesus Christ should be leading the way in financial integrity. Pastors and Christian leaders should be providing answers regarding how to handle money and not gaining headlines through practicing unethical behaviors. We serve the King of Kings. We work as unto the Lord, so why shouldn't we be the best in the industry?

Every church or ministry receives and spends money. How we do those two primary activities will reflect our financial integrity. Do we have the proper controls in place to discourage fraud? Do we even know what controls are necessary? If not, we are unarmed in a gun battle, and that is always unwise. (Can I still write gun in our current political climate?)

The Church is populated with humans. Humans are subject to temptation. Money, and often large quantities of it, is a major temptation to many humans. What are we doing to help those that deal with money to resist or overcome this temptation? How do we know if they are being successful in their struggles? Financial integrity demands that we answer these questions. If we fail to do so, we may find our ministries on the front page of the newspaper, or the subject of thousands of Tweets. We may lose them entirely.

Do not despair; there is good news! Churches and Christian ministries can implement policies and procedures that will keep honest people honest. These practices do not have to cost much. In fact, most of them cost nothing at all. Okay, there is the cost of time, and perhaps overcoming the resistance to changing improper behaviors, but these are not financial in nature.

Where do we begin to change? First, there must be a desire to *want to* change. Will you embrace Glenn's challenge to become the leader in financial integrity in your community? Even if no one ever asks you a question about how you handle your finances, you can and should excel. We serve the King of the Universe and anything less than our best is too little and unacceptable.

Second, will you pursue education to learn how to become an excellent leader in financial integrity? No one knows everything, so we all need help. Glenn is a Certified Fraud Examiner. The fact that we have to have such people in the Christian world is disheartening, but leaving that aside for a moment, he, and those like him, have a lot of wisdom to share.

In the interest of full disclosure, I help teach along with Glenn at The Institute of Church Management. I have been in full time, paid ministry for over thirty years. For eleven of those years I was the administrator of a large church in my city, and for about the last twenty years, I have served as a senior pastor of my own church. I am therefore somewhat familiar with the inner workings of the church.

While serving as an administrator, I studied and passed the CFP (Certified Financial Planner) professional designation exam. Since becoming a senior pastor, I have completed my Masters degree, a Doctorate and a Ph.D. I know a little bit about studying and learning as well. When I challenge people to keep on learning I am speaking from a position of experience. We must study and we must grow, learn and adapt.

So, back to my second point: will you pursue the education necessary to learn what needs to be accomplished to protect your ministry? If you will not, who will then? If you will not become the leader in integrity in your ministry, who will? Who should it be if not you?

There are tools available to assist you in your pursuit of excellence in integrity. The Institute of Church Management has plenty of them. The National Association of Church Business Administrators and The Evangelical Council for Financial Accountability do as well.

Regarding financial accountability and integrity, Jesus' words still remain true – "ask and you will receive, seek and you will find". Lead with integrity and you soon will be followed. I know the last words are not Jesus', but they are true nonetheless.

I will leave you with two questions of my own – Will we lead in integrity? If not, why not?

Typical Financial Statement Services From Accountants/CPAs

COMPILATION

Preparing financial statements where no assurance as to reliability is provided

What are compilation services?

Compilation services can be provided by public accountants or certified public accountants (CPAs). The latter is required to comply with standards promulgated by the American Institute of Certified Public Accountants (AICPA). Through compilation services, an accountant or CPA prepares monthly, quarterly or annual financial statements. However, the accountant or CPA offers no assurance as to whether material, or significant changes are necessary for the financial statements to be in conformity with generally accepted accounting principles (or another comprehensive basis of accounting such as modified cash basis). During a compilation, the information provided by the organization's management is simply arranged into conventional financial statement format. No reconciliations, analyses, queries, tests, re-computations, confirmation or examination of supporting documents is required. If the CPA becomes aware that the data is inaccurate or incomplete, management is requested to make the necessary changes.

What does a compilation entail?

A compilation does require the accountant or CPA to be familiar with the accounting principles and practices common to the industry and how organization records its transactions. Once the financial statements are compiled, the accountant or CPA should read them and consider whether they are in appropriate form and free from obvious misstatements. The CPA then issues a standard report that states that the financial statements were complied, but since they were not reviewed or audited, no opinion is expressed. See Appendix B-1 for an example. A compilation does not include any focus on fraud.

Compilation standards permit an accountant to compile financial statements without footnotes or a statement of cash flows if the report letter clearly indicates the omission. The accountant does not have to be independent as long as that is disclosed in the accountant's report.

When is a compilation enough?

Compiled financial statements may be adequate to internal purposes or when external readers have an intimate knowledge of the organization and its operations or have sufficient influence to obtain additional that may be needed. If the financial statement users need some degree of assurance as to the reliability of the financial statements, a CPA would need to be engaged to perform a review or an audit.

REVIEW

Financial statements where limited assurance as to reliability is provided

<u>What are review services?</u>

Here an organization engages a CPA to review its financial statements in accordance with standards established by the AICPA and issue a report that provides limited assurance that material changes to the financial statements are not necessary, i.e., negative assurance. See Appendix B-2 for an example. With respect to reliability and assurance, a review falls somewhere between a compilation which provides no assurance and the extensive assurance of an audit. Only a licensed CPA is permitted to review or audit financial statements. While the CPA may compile the financial statements here also, they are management's statements and management must assume responsibility for them. Two factors distinguish a review from a compilation. First, the CPA must be independent and all appropriate disclosures (including cash flows) must be included in the reviewed financial statements.

<u>What does a review entail?</u>

The CPA must obtain a working knowledge of the industry and acquire information on key aspects of the organization, including operating methods, products, services and material transactions with related parties. The CPA will then make inquiries concerning such financial statement related matters as accounting principles and practices, record keeping practices, accounting policies, actions of the board of directors, changes in business activities, and <u>knowledge of fraud or suspected fraud that could have a material effect on the financial statements</u> among other things. In addition, the CPA will apply analytical procedures designed to identify unusual items or trends in the financial statements that may need an explanation. Management will be required to make certain written representations. Based upon these procedures, the CPA may recommend that changes be made to the amounts or disclosures in the financial statements so that they are in compliance with generally accepted accounting principles or another comprehensive basis of accounting. In summary, a review is only designed to determine whether the financial statements "make sense" without applying audit-type tests.

<u>When is a review the right choice?</u>

Reviewed financial statements can give the board and management some limited assurance. Reviewed financial statements may be adequate to external users such as donors or lenders, when the external readers <u>do not</u> have an intimate knowledge of the organization and its operations or sufficient influence to obtain additional that may be needed. Under these circumstances, a review engagement may be sufficient. If the financial statement users need positive assurance as to the reliability of the financial statements, a CPA would need to be engaged to perform an audit.

AUDIT

Financial statements where the highest level of assurance as to reliability is provided

What are audit services?

When an organization engages a CPA to audit its financial statements, the expectation is that the CPA will perform an audit in accordance with generally accepted auditing standards established by the AICPA (and government agencies, if applicable) and issue a report that provides the highest level of assurance that the financial statements are presented fairly in conformity with generally accepted accounting principles or other comprehensive basis of accounting. See Appendix B-3 for a sample report.

In an audit, as in a review, the CPA must be independent of the client and the financial statements must include all required statements and disclosures.

What does an audit entail?

The first step is for the CPA to communicate with the client's governing board (or its finance or audit committee) re: the nature and scope of the engagement. This is done because the auditor is engaged by and reports to the governing body and not management. The next phase includes a significant amount of data gathering and planning. This phase will include documenting the organization's accounting controls (internal and third-party) and performing limited (or extensive tests) to determine whether the controls are implemented as described (or are working as designed), depending on the amount of reliance the CPA intends to place on the controls. In addition, this phase requires the auditor to assess the risk of material misstatements in significant accounts or transaction cycles as determined by knowledge of the client, the industry, the economy and many other factors. These factors include "business" and fraud risks identified by management and the governing board. The audit team also spends time together analyzing the data gathered, internal control risks identified, client personnel qualifications, prior experience with the client, and brainstorms about how and where fraud (both misappropriation of assets and falsification of financial) data might occur. Based upon this and other data, the audit team tailors its audit plan and procedures to focus on those areas identified as higher risk. The objective is to reduce the risk that the financial statements and disclosures are materially misstated.

The next phase of an audit is to gather evidence on the reliability of the financial statements. This entails confirmations with third parties such as banks, donors, vendors, lenders, attorneys and others as well as re-computations, observations (especially inventory), analytics, inquiries, and examination of documents, among other things. In addition, the audit team is required to interview selected employees regarding fraud, the suspicion of fraud, areas where fraud could occur, internal fraud risk assessment and to examine selected journal entries and estimates for reasonableness and absence of bias. The audit team will also perform other selected procedures directed at identifying fraud. While an audit is planned and conducted with sensitivity to the possibility of fraud, it is the responsibility of the governing body and management to protect the organization and detect fraud if it occurs.

Remember, an audit provides a reasonable level of assurance that the financial statements are free of material error and fraud, but does not provide a guarantee of either. In addition to the auditor's report on the financial statements, the engagement should include a letter to the governing board summarizing the engagement and its results including significant deficiencies and/or material weaknesses in internal controls. The engagement should also include the CPA's comments and recommendations for improving the organization's financial operations and controls.

When is an audit the best choice?

Many events can warrant the level of assurance an audit provides; here are some:

1. Solicitation or awarding of a foundation grant
2. Contributions exceeding a specified amount
3. Participating in federated fundraising
4. Being an affiliate, chapter or accredited organization
5. Issuing securities such as church bonds
6. Expending more than $500,000 of federal funding

7. State filing requirements where funds are solicited
8. Required by the organization's by-laws
9. Required by a lender
10. Assistance to accounting and financial personnel
11. Demonstration of good stewardship and integrity to donors, members and other constituents.

An audit requires a nonprofit organization to commit substantial resources in the form of money, time and cooperation with the auditor. The governing body should weigh the needs of the organization against the required commitment of resources before selecting this option.
*Adapted in part from the AICPA brochure *"Understanding Compilation, Review and Audit."*

Ministry Anti-Fraud Self-Evaluation Checklist

The checklist that follows will assist you in determining both your current risks and a roadmap to dealing with any exposures you discover. As you work though each category, check which "state" your ministry currently resides in and then total up the results on the last page. Don't be discouraged if your ministry ends up high in the wrong categories. The point of the exercise is to help strengthen areas of weakness and those can only be discovered by working through the process.

While no amount of internal controls or policies can guarantee that your ministry will not suffer fraud, we can, and must, do the best job possible to limit the opportunities for its occurrence.

By making the changes necessary to move our ministries from being a Fire Hazard to becoming Fireproof, we have taken some excellent steps!

Gather your ministry, leadership and financial teams and fill out the form looking for ways to strengthen your ministry. The ministry you save might just be your own!

Fire Rating

☑ Fireproof Checklist

Cash Disbursements			
	Fire Hazard	**Fire Resistant**	**☑ Fireproof**
Check Signatures	☐ We only have one person sign checks. On larger checks, we have two people sign. We may utilize signature stamps that are held by the person preparing the checks.	☐ We normally require two signatures on our checks, but sometimes we only have one signer available so we make exceptions.	☐ Two signatures are required on every check – no exceptions. We have "requires 2 signatures" printed on our checks to help the bank enforce this. It also reminds check signers that two signatures are required.
	☐ We require one check signature on some or most of our checks.	☐ We have two check signers, but we sometimes allow relatives, and staff who are in subordinate relationships, to sign checks together.	☐ Our check signers are not related to each other, and checks are not signed by a staff member and his/her supervisor. As often as possible, we have at least one check signer sign most of the checks so they can check for trends and other issues.
	☐ Because our check signers are sometimes unavailable we occasionally leave a few signed/blank checks available in case there's an emergency.	☐ We don't allow signed/blank checks, but in an unusual circumstance that justifies it, we will pre-sign a check.	☐ We never, ever, sign blank checks in advance for any reason.
Separation of Duties	☐ The same person prepares and signs checks.	☐ The person who prepares the checks signs them along with someone else.	☐ We make sure the person who generates checks does not sign them.
Check Documentation	☐ We try to have supporting documentation for all checks but it doesn't always work.	☐ We have good documentation on most things, but sometimes it's attached after the checks are signed.	☐ We have clear backup documentation for every check attached to the check, before it's signed.

Cash Disbursements (continued)			
	Fire Hazard	Fire Resistant	☑ Fireproof
Manual Checks	☐ We write all manual checks.	☐ We do most of our checks on a computerized accounting system, but write several manual checks per month.	☐ We have eliminated the use of "emergency" manual checks since we're on a computerized accounting system. It helps improve our record keeping.
Expense Reimbursements	☐ One person approves our expense reimbursements.	☐ Our Finance Committee approves *all* expense reimbursements. It's become somewhat of a formality.	☐ We ensure correct handling of timely expense reimbursements. This includes a formal accountable reimbursement plan with proper documentation.
Voided Checks	☐ We throw away voided checks to make sure they're never used.	☐ We write "void" on the checks and then shred them. Our computer system keeps track of which checks have been voided.	☐ Our voided checks are marked "Void" and kept on file in a secure location.
Payroll			
Compensation Changes	☐ We don't keep track of changes in payroll.	☐ Someone on the Personnel Committee keeps all of that information.	☐ All compensation changes are approved by the personnel committee and documented with all necessary details and secured in the personnel file.
Compensation Processing	☐ We're not really doing the withholding thing for our employees. We just write checks like a 1099 situation.	☐ We process all employee payments through payroll unless it's a bonus, special gift, or benevolence situation.	☐ All compensation is processed through the payroll system, including love offerings, special gifts, and Christmas bonuses.
Payroll Documentation	☐ I'm not entirely sure what a W-4, W-9, and an I-9 are and when to use each.	☐ We have W-4s for our employees but we don't have I-9s for everyone. W-9s??	☐ A current W-4 and I-9 is on file for every staff member. W-9s are obtained for all contract laborers before payments are made to them.

Payroll (continued)			
	Fire Hazard	**Fire Resistant**	☑ **Fireproof**
Housing Allowance	☐ We allow our staff to change their housing allowance allocation throughout the year as their circumstances change. It's not approved by anyone or it isn't included in our board minutes.	☐ We always approve our ministers' housing allowances in the board minutes but on a rare occasion they are approved retroactively.	☐ We require our ministerial staff to complete housing allowance forms each year and have the amounts formally approved in the board meeting minutes by December 31 for the coming year. Changes are always approved prospectively.
Compen-sation Laws	☐ We pay all of our staff a straight salary regardless of hours worked.	☐ We pay our ministers a straight salary and we pay all other staff by the hour, and we pay time and a half for overtime.	☐ We follow all federal wage and hour regulations relating to exempt and non-exempt staff.
	☐ We tell our staff not to work overtime, so if they do, we only have to pay them straight time.	☐ We pay overtime only for staff who are paid by the hour. We sometimes allow them to volunteer their time if they work more than 40 hrs/week.	☐ As required, we pay overtime to non-exempt staff for all hours worked, regardless of whether they are hourly or salaried.
Payroll Taxes	☐ We don't withhold taxes on non-ministerial staff but we pay them extra so they can pay in taxes themselves.	☐ We properly withhold state and federal taxes and then remit them when we have the funds available.	☐ We always have correct and timely filing of all payroll taxes and reports, including quarterly 941 payroll tax forms, annual W-2 and W-3 forms, etc.
	☐ We remit our payroll tax withholdings when we have enough cash.	☐ Since we always have a hard time paying payroll taxes on time, we only collect and remit federal payroll taxes.	☐ All federal, state, and local payroll taxes are properly withheld and remitted on a timely basis.
W-2s & 1099's	☐ We process payroll as W-2 payments unless someone only works a few hours a month.	☐ We properly issue 1099s to all contract laborers unless we don't have their social security number.	☐ We ensure correct classification of employees vs. contractors and the timely distribution of W-2s and 1099s.

Appendix - Self-Evaluation Checklist

Bank & Investment Account Management			
	Fire Hazard	Fire Resistant	☑ Fireproof
Bank Accounts	☐ We allow each committee in the church to maintain its own bank account so they can keep tabs on their own money. We have at least one account not listed on our monthly financial statements.	☐ Only our Finance Committee is authorized to oversee the several designated bank accounts within the church.	☐ We maintain a minimum number of bank accounts and keep track of designated funds through the accounting system. Committees are issued reports on a monthly basis regarding their funds.
Bank Reconciliations	☐ Our checking account is balanced but we don't do a formal bank reconciliation.	☐ One of the persons who creates or signs checks or makes deposits is responsible for reconciling the bank account.	☐ Monthly bank reconciliations are made by someone not responsible for writing checks or making deposits.
Bank & Investment Accounts	☐ We reconcile our bank account monthly and adjust the investment account balance when we sell or purchase investments.	☐ We tie our bank and investment account reconciliations to the GL just before preparing our quarterly Finance Committee report.	☐ Bank and investment account balances are reconciled on a monthly basis and matched to the penny to the GL.
Offerings, Deposits, & Contribution Recordkeeping			
Offering Count Guidelines	☐ Our offering counting committee is trained how to do their job, but the Finance Team isn't aware of their procedures.	☐ The people involved in counting the offering are taught by those who already who know how to do it. One of our Finance Team members used to be involved in counting.	☐ Written instructions are made available to everyone involved in counting the offering and to those who have oversight responsibility for the finances.
Offering Counting	☐ When the offering is counted, there is always someone nearby.	☐ We always require two people to count the offering but we allow one person to leave the room during the counting.	☐ At least two to three are actively involved in counting the offering.
	☐ We've had the same people counting offering together for years.	☐ We rotate our offering counters when they no longer want to be on the team and we have to find someone new.	☐ We require our offering counters to serve 1-3 times per month on a rotating basis-not always with the same team.

169

Offerings, Deposits, & Contribution Recordkeeping (continued)			
	Fire Hazard	**Fire Resistant**	☑ **Fireproof**
Offering Counting	☐ Some of our counters are related to each other.	☐ Some of our counters are related to those who have responsibility for other finance duties (prepare/sign checks, do bank reconciliation, etc.)	☐ No one in our offering counting team is related to each other or to anyone else with responsibilities for finance.
	☐ Offering count records are not signed by the counters.	☐ Some or most of the offering count records are initialed by the counters.	☐ All offering count records are signed by all counters involved when finalized.
	☐ Deposit slips are taken with the deposit to the bank.	☐ Deposit slips are taken to the bank and the bank sends a copy of it back to us.	☐ One copy of the deposit slip is delivered with the deposit to the bank while the other one is kept with another responsible person who doesn't go to the bank.
Offering Reports	☐ If there are errors in our offering, we know that when the bank sends us a deposit correction notice.	☐ The accountant matches the offering report to the list of donations entered in the data base.	☐ The accountant matches the offering report to (1) the deposit slip processed by the bank, (2) to the contribution data base, and (3) to the GL.
Security of Offerings	☐ After the offering is collected it is stored in a lockable filing cabinet under some files. Only two people have a key to this cabinet.	☐ We deposit our offerings in a drop safe that only the officers of the Finance Committee have access to.	☐ Offerings are deposited in a drop safe that requires two separate individuals to open. No single person has access to the funds.
Financial Reporting			
Financial Statements	☐ We produce a statement of income and expenses every month.	☐ The Finance Committee receives an income and expense comparison report once a quarter.	☐ The board or committee with fiscal responsibility receives a Statement of Activities (Income Statement) report monthly.

Financial Reporting (continued)	Fire Hazard	Fire Resistant	☑ Fireproof
Financial Statements	☐ We do not use a budget.	☐ We have a budget but don't use it very well.	☐ Those with fiscal responsibility review a monthly comparison of income & expenses to budget monthly.
	☐ Financials are prepared when the person responsible has time.	☐ Financials are prepared within at least six weeks of the reporting period ending.	☐ Financial reports are prepared and distributed at least by the 20th of each month.
General			
Audits	☐ Our organization has never had an audit.	☐ We have had an audit but it has been a while since we had one.	☐ We are on a schedule of regular audits.
Treasurer Role	☐ The Pastor or a pastor's relative serves as our Treasurer.	☐ A paid staff member, or a relative of a paid staff member, serves as the Treasurer.	☐ We have a Treasurer who is not a paid staff member and is not related to any paid staff member.
Sales Tax Exemption	☐ We don't have a sales tax exemption letter.	☐ We have a sales tax exempt letter but don't use it all the time.	☐ A tax exempt letter is used for all purchases.
Insurance	☐ We have had the same insurance coverage for years.	☐ We review our insurance coverage whenever we are prompted by a major change in our ministry.	☐ We perform an annual review of all insurance coverage and cost.
	☐ We do not carry worker's compensation insurance.	☐ I'm not sure if we carry worker's comp insurance.	☐ We carry worker's compensation insurance.
Records Retention	☐ We just keep everything for a really long time!	☐ We might have a records retention policy but don't really take the time to follow it.	☐ We have a records retention policy. We review files annually and take appropriate action according to our written retention schedule.

Our Ministry's Score	Fire Hazard	Fire Resistant	Fireproof!
	_____	_____	_____

"My organization's rating wasn't bad! Many of my answers were in the Fireproof column. So I assume that means we're okay?"

What steps need to be taken to move all aspects of our organization toward the Fireproof rating?

_____

_____

_____

_____

Sample Counting Agreements/Forms
Biblical Ministry Description
for Offering Counters

__Responsible To:__ _____(name), _____(title)

__Purpose of Ministry:__
The purpose of the Offering Counter Team is to provide accurate, consistent, confidential and timely processing of all donations and monetary gifts to the church.

__Duties:__
Follow offering counting procedures as outlined in a separate document, including:
- Pre-service setup of supplies
- Collect offerings during service
- Sort, count, and record offerings and donation credit
- Maintain names/lists for special offerings
- Take deposit to bank
- Provide contribution report and documentation to _____ as required

__Desired Results:__
- Feeling of trust / security / confidence from church members and visitors
- Good, accurate financial records
- Confidentiality of donor records
- Assist the Treasurer by ensuring good information is fed into the General Ledger

__Time Commitment:__
- ___ to ___minutes per week

Gifts, Skills, Talents, & Qualifications:

Qualifications:
- An active Church Member for __ months
- Regular, consistent giver

Gifts, Skills, Talents:
- Spiritual gift of administration
- Responsible
- Organization skills
- Attention to detail
- Financial integrity on a personal level
- Ability to *consistently* maintain confidentiality
- Assertiveness to bring up anything that "doesn't feel right" to the lead counter or senior church leader

Offering Team Confidentiality Agreement
(Church / Organization Name)

Thank you for agreeing to serve in the ministry position of Offering Counting Team member. We are honored that you are willing to use your spiritual gift of administration to assist the Church. It is our goal to strive for the highest level of integrity as we are entrusted to be stewards of the Lord's finances in the local body of Christ.

This agreement serves to clarify expectations of confidentiality in your role as a member of the Offering Counting Team. Confidential information is defined as: all information obtained through performing offering counting and related administrative duties. This includes, but is not limited to, names and addresses of donors, amount of any individual donations, individual giving patterns, bank account information, etc. By signing below, I agree that I will strictly maintain the confidentiality of all information as defined above.

_____   _____   _____

Printed Name   Signature   Date

Cash Counting Sheet - Counter #1

Type of Count: ☐ Loose ☐ Envelopes ☐ Activities/Fees

Date:_____

CURRENCY			COIN		
$100.00			Dollars		
$50.00			Fifty Cent		
$20.00			Quarters		
$10.00			Dimes		
$5.00			Nickles		
$1.00			Pennies		
TOTAL			TOTAL		

TOTAL

Counter Signature:_____

- - - - - - - - - - - [Fold Here] - - - - - - - - - - - -

Cash Counting Sheet - Counter #2

CURRENCY			COIN		
$100.00			Dollars		
$50.00			Fifty Cent		
$20.00			Quarters		
$10.00			Dimes		
$5.00			Nickles		
$1.00			Pennies		
TOTAL			TOTAL		

TOTAL

Counter Signature:_____

Loose Check Log
(for Contribution Credit Only)

Date:

Name	ID Number	Check Number	#3110 Gen.Offering	Other Description (Acct. #)	Other Amount	Total

Counter Signature: _____

Sample Policies

Crisis Communication Team & Policy

Accurate and informed communications during a crisis is of utmost importance and may have a positive impact on congregational reputation and support following a crisis. The following guidelines will prepare you to convey the right message to the congregation, community, and media, thus reducing the risks of hearsay and rumors.

1. Anticipate a Crisis. By being proactive, the church can respond to internal crisis (scams, criminal activity, moral failure, etc.) and external crisis (floods, tornados, hurricanes, fire, etc.) without the added pressure of having to ask, "What now?"
2. Assemble a Crisis Communication Team. Generally this will include key leadership (Pastors, Elders, Select Staff, Chairman of Deacons, Treasurer, Building & Grounds leadership). Questions to ask include:
   a. Who should be on your church crisis communication team?
   b. How often should the team meet? (Annually is recommended.)
3. Ascertain the Spokesperson(s). It is critical that the church have one person responsible for communicating to the congregation, community, and media. Although the senior pastor is generally the spokesperson, it is necessary to have at least one other trained spokesperson in case of pastoral absence or the communication involves the pastor.

  a. The person communicating must be on the communication team, thus having the correct understanding of the situation.

  b. The person must understand what to say, what not to say, and how to say it.

  c. Use written statements, and never "shoot from the hip." Seek to convey a brutal optimism that is honest and conveys hope.

4. Develop "holding statements." In the case of a crisis, holding statements are used until the crisis communication team can develop fuller communications. Have several holding statements available in writing before a crisis hits is wise. Samples might include:

  a. We have implemented our crisis response plan, which places our highest priority on our congregation.

  b. Our prayers are with those affected by this event. Additional information will be supplied when available, and posted on our website.

  c. The church is actively cooperating with authorities in their investigation of the allegations.

5. Identify outlets for communication. In a crisis, every member is a "PR representative" for your church. Provide them with accurate information, even if it is simply the holding statement. Ensure people know where to go for updated information (website, social media site, contact person, etc.).

6. Communicate follow-up messages. These communications should share appropriate facts in

the form of a statement. Be sure to convey any appreciations (such as to disaster relief or thank you for your prayers). Avoid Q&A sessions during the crisis period.

7. Post-Event Analysis. In the after mass of a crisis, it is tempting to catch one's breath. However, this is an opportunity for the crisis communication team to reflect on three questions. What was done well? What could be done differently? What have we learned? After this meeting, it is appropriate for the crisis communication team to conduct a Q&A session with the congregation.

Sample Whistle-Blower Policy

GENERAL POLICY STATEMENT

Church/Ministry name is responsible for establishing the cultural environment, training employees, volunteers, and board members regarding whistle-blower policies in support of the church's anti-fraud policies and conflict of interest policies. This whistle-blower policy is intended to provide parameters, definition, procedures, and protection to those involved in the discovery and/or subsequent reporting of violations of the church's anti-fraud or conflict of interest policies.

It is the church's policy that there is zero tolerance for actions that subvert, decrease, or otherwise prevents or impairs this policy to fulfill its intended purpose.

DEFINITION OF A WHISTLE-BLOWER

A whistle-blower is defined as any individual, inside or outside the organization, who provides substantiated information regarding an employee, volunteer, vendor, contractor, consultant, board member, or other organization doing business with or who is associated with the church and is in violation of stated church's anti-fraud or conflict of interest policies.

WHO IS INCLUDED IN THE WHISTLE-BLOWER

Any employee, volunteer, vendor, contractor, consultant, board member, or other organization doing business with or who is associated with the church.

REPORTING RESPONSIBILITIES AND SAFEGUARDS

Any known or suspected violations of the church's anti-fraud or conflict of interest policies should be reported immediately upon discovery to the Senior Pastor and the Chairman of the Board.

It is the responsibility of every board member, employee, or volunteer to report, preferably in writing, discovered or suspected violations of the church's anti-fraud or conflict of interest policies.

No reporting party, who in good faith reports such a matter, will suffer harassment, retaliation, or other adverse consequences. Any board member, employee, or volunteer who harasses or retaliates against the party who reported such a matter in good faith is subject to discipline up to and including termination of employment or removal from the board. Any allegation that proves to have been made maliciously or knowingly to be false will be viewed as a serious disciplinary offense against the accuser.

CONFIDENTIALITY

Discovered or suspected matters can be reported anonymously or on a confidential basis. Anonymous allegations will be investigated, but consideration will be given to seriousness of the issue, its credibility, and the likelihood of confirming the allegation from other reliable sources. In the case of allegations made on a confidential basis, every effort will be made to keep the identity of the reporting party secret, consistent with the need to conduct an adequate and fair investigation.

Allegations will not be discussed with anyone other than those who have a legitimate need to know. It is important to protect the rights of the persons accused, to avoid damaging their reputation should they be found innocent, and to protect the organization from potential liability.

INVESTIGATION PROCEDURES

The Chair of the Board or their delegate will investigate all allegations on a timely basis. The investigation may include but is not limited t examining, copying and/or removing all or a portion of the contents of files, desks, cabinets, and other facilities of the organization without prior knowledge or consent of any individual who may use or have custody of such items or facilities when it is within the scope of the investigation.

The reporting party must not attempt to personally conduct investigations, interviews, or interrogations related to the alleged fraudulent activity.

RESOLUTION PROCEDURES

The results of the investigation will be reported to the Board of Directors. Actions taken against the perpetrator of alleged policy violations will be determined by the Board with potential consultation with legal counsel.

CURRENT CONTACT INFORMATION

Senior Pastor:

Xxxxxx
Xxxxxxxx
xxxxxxxxxx

Chair of the Board:

Xxxxx
Xxxxxxx

<u>Sample Credit Card Policy & Agreement</u>

By issuing you a credit card, we are demonstrating our trust in you. You are empowered as a responsible agent to safeguard our assets. Your signature below is verification that you have read and agree to comply with the following responsibilities. It also acknowledges that you have received card #XXX-XXXX-XXX.

1. I understand the card is for organization approved purchases only and I agree not to charge personal purchases.

2. Improper use of this card can be considered misappropriation of funds. This may result in disciplinary action up to and including termination of employment.

3. If the card is lost or stolen, I will immediately notify the bank. I will confirm the telephone call by written correspondence to the program administrator.

4. I agree to surrender the card immediately upon termination of employment, whether for retirement, voluntary, or involuntary reasons.

5. The card is issued in my name. I will not allow any other person to use the card. I am responsible for any and all charges against the card.

6. All charges will be billed directly to and paid directly by our organization. The bank cannot accept any monies from me directly; therefore any personal charges billed to the organization could be considered misappropriation of funds.

7. As the card is not my own, I understand that I may be required to comply with internal control procedures designed to protect assets. This may include being asked to produce the card to validate its existence and account number. I will be required to produce receipts and statements to audit its use.

8. I will receive a monthly statement, which will report all activity during the statement period. Since I am responsible for all charges (but not payment) on the card, I will work with the program administrator to resolve any charge discrepancies.

9. To meet IRS and our organization's standards, original corresponding receipts will accompany each credit card statement and include in that documentation the following substantiation requirements: business purpose for the expense, names or titles if paying for others, dates of travel.

10. I understand a credit card is not automatically provided to all employees or volunteers. Assignment is based on my need to purchase materials for the organization and/or to provide for organization travel. My card may be revoked based on change of assignment, need, or violation of this

agreement. I understand that the card is not an entitlement nor reflective of title or position.

_____   _____

Cardholder Signature   Program Administrator
                              Signature

_____   _____

Cardholder Printed Name   Date

_____   _____

Program Administrator Printed Name   Date

Sample Anti-Fraud Policy

GENERAL POLICY STATEMENT

Church/Ministry Name is responsible for establishing the cultural environment, training employees, volunteers, and board members, assessing fraud risks, implementing internal controls, and monitoring activities designed to prevent and detect misappropriation of organization's assets and intentional material misrepresentation of organization's financial or other data or other actions constituting fraud. It is management's responsibility to communicate this policy to all board members, employees, and volunteers and their responsibility to comply with this policy.

It is the church's policy that there is zero tolerance for actions constituting fraud.

DEFINITION OF FRAUD

Actions defined as fraud include, but are not limited to:

- Theft of cash, securities, merchandise, equipment, supplies, or other assets.

- Unauthorized use of organization employees, property, credit cards, cell phones, or other resources.

- Submission of personal or fictitious employee expenses for reimbursement or fictitious or inflated vendor invoices or payroll records for payment.

- Receiving kickbacks or other unauthorized personal benefits from vendors or others.

- Forgery or fraudulent alteration of any check, bank draft, statement, billing, record, form, report, return, or other financial document.

- Intentional material misclassification or misrepresentation of revenues, expenses, costs or other data in financial statements, reports, regulatory returns, applications, or other communications.

- Intentional failure to disclose material related party transactions, noncompliance with lender requirements, or donor/grantor restrictions or other required disclosure matters.

- Intentional improper use or disclosure of confidential donor, client/customer, employee, or organization proprietary information.

- Any violation of copyright or licensing laws.

- Any other illegal or unethical activity

WHO IS INCLUDED IN THE ANTI-FRAUD POLICY

The anti fraud policy applies to fraud or suspected fraud by board members, employees, volunteers, vendors, contractors, consultants, and others doing business with the church or its subsidiaries.

REPORTING RESPONSIBILITIES AND SAFEGUARDS

It is the responsibility of every board member, employee, or volunteer to report, preferably in writing, discovered or suspected unethical or fraudulent activity immediately to the Senior Pastor and/or the Chairman of the Board.

No reporting party who in good faith reports such a matter will suffer harassment, retaliation, or other adverse consequences. Any board member, employee, or volunteer who harasses or retaliates against the party who reported such a matter in good faith is subject to discipline up to and including termination of employment, or removal from board. Additionally, no board member, employee, or volunteer will be adversely affected because they refuse to carry out a directive which constitutes fraud or is a violation of state or federal law.

Any allegation that proves to have been made maliciously or knowingly to be false will be viewed as a serious disciplinary offense against the accuser.

CONFIDENTIALITY

Discovered or suspected matters can be reported anonymously or on a confidential basis. Anonymous allegations will be investigated, but consideration will be given to seriousness of the issue, its credibility and the likelihood of confirming the allegation from other reliable sources. In the case of allegations made on a confidential basis, every effort will be made to keep the identity of the reporting party secret, consistent with the need to conduct an adequate and fair investigation.

Allegations will not be discussed with anyone other than those who have a legitimate need to know. It is important to protect the rights of the persons accused, to avoid damaging their reputation should they be found innocent, and to protect the organization from potential liability.

INVESTIGATION PROCEDURES

The Chair of the Board or their delegate will investigate all allegations on a timely basis. The investigation may include but is not limited to examining, copying and/or removing all or a portion of the contents of computers, computer files, disks, tapes, other electronic storage devices, files, desks, cabinets, and other facilities of the organization without prior knowledge or consent of any individual who may use or have custody of such items or facilities when it is within the scope of the investigation.

The reporting party must not attempt to personally conduct investigations, interviews, or interrogations related to the alleged fraudulent activity.

RESOLUTION PROCEDURES

The results of the investigation will be reported to the Board of Directors. Actions taken against the perpetrator of alleged fraud will be determined by the Board with potential consultation with legal counsel.

CURRENT CONTACT INFORMATION

Senior Pastor:
Xxxxx
Xxxxxx
Xxxxxxxx

Chair of the Board:
Xxxxx
Xxxxxx
Xxxxxxxx

General Guidelines for Record Retention

Nonprofit organizations are often confronted with the challenge of records management and retention. It is not unusual for convenience and limited space to drive these decisions; however, a variety of government regulations and best practices should be considered and lead to a formal policy that is consistently followed. Such a policy should be understood and approved by the organization's governance board and leadership. Organizations have a responsibility to protect records in both the retention and destruction processes. Companies that specialize in the destruction of documents should be consulted to properly shred and dispose of paper copies as well as purge electronic files from the server and backup devices.

In some situations, a records retention policy covering the disposal of records should be immediately suspended. The destruction of records should cease when:

- the organization is served with any subpoena or request for documents.
- the organization is subject to a governmental investigation or audit.
- the commencement of any litigation against or concerning the organization occurs.

Miller Management Systems, LLC (a/k/a MMS, LLC) offers the following recommended time frames that each of the listed records and documents should be retained.

The following guidelines apply to both physical and electronic documents:

Accounting Records	3 years	7 years	Permanently
Invoices (after payment)	X		
Monthly financial reports	X		
Budgets	X		
Accounts payable/receivable ledgers & schedules		X	
Employee Expense reports & logs		X	
Bank statements and reconciliations		X	
Cancelled checks		X	
General Ledgers			X
Audit reports			X
End-of-year financial statements			X
Checks used for important payments, such as taxes, property, etc.			X
Contribution Records			
Contribution envelopes	X		
Donor contribution receipts		X	
Contribution ledgers & schedules		X	
Payroll and Personnel Records			
Employment/Personnel Records		X	
Payroll Registers		X	
W-2 and W-4 forms		X	
Proof of deductions		X	
Property Records			
Leases			X
Service contracts (after termination)	X		
Property Insurance			X
Real Estate Records			X
Tax Records			
Tax bills, receipts, statements		X	
Payroll Tax Records		X	
Sales/use tax records		X	
Tax exemption letter			X
Tax and information returns			X

IRS examinations			X
Corporate Records			
Contracts		X	
Committee minutes and bylaws			X
Articles of Incorporation			X
Insurance records			X
Electronic Records			
E-mail, PDF files, electronic document files	Retention depends on the subject matter.		

Helpful Links

http://www.mmsmidwest.com/institute-for-church-management/
Provider of the *Fireproofing Your Ministry* DVD workshop and other Christian management training.

http://www.mmsmidwest.com/ Accounting, payroll, operational audits, consulting and training for non-profits and churches.

http://www.acfe.com/ The Association of Certified Fraud Examiners. Great place for additional resources in learning about and combating fraud.

http://www.ecfa.org/ The Evangelical Council of Financial Accountability. The Good Housekeeping seal for Christian ministries in how they handle money.

http://www.nacba.net/Pages/Home.aspx The National Association of Church Business Administrators. Excellent resources for all things related to church administration.

http://www.churchmutual.com All manner of insurance for churches.

https://www.guideone.com/ Church insurance.

http://www.mbts.edu/ Midwestern Baptist Theological Seminary.

http://www.kellerowens.com/not-for-profit-organizations - Many excellent reports, surveys and tools for churches and ministries from a great CPA firm.

Author Bio's

Glenn A. Miller

Glenn has served the Church in multiple capacities since the mid-1980s. Glenn has been a church administrator with two different ministries, a director of Financial and IT Services, a CFO of two seminaries, and currently is the president of Miller Management Systems, LLC in Kansas City, Missouri, a public accounting firm that specializes in serves for churches and non-profits. In addition to assisting over 1,400 churches and other non-profit organizations with accounting, administration, and consultation, Glenn founded the Institute for Church Management which has trained hundreds of leaders in effective administration. Glenn is a highly awarded senior adjunct professor for Baker University for 20 years, and has also taught at Sterling College and Avila University. Glenn is a Certified DiSC Personality Assessment Trainer, a Certified Fraud Examiner, and has completed his MBA from The University of Missouri-KC. He is currently completing his Doctorate in Educational Ministries. Glenn has been married to Kim since 1981 and has four adult children: Chris, Jon, Beth, and Ben; and, Anysia, the first granddaughter!

Jeffrey A. Klick

Dr. Jeff Klick has been in fulltime ministry for over thirty-four years (since 1981). He currently serves as the senior pastor at Hope Family Fellowship in Kansas City, Kansas, a church he planted in 1993. Dr. Klick married his high school sweetheart, Leslie, in May of 1975. They have three adult children and ten grandchildren. Dr. Klick loves to learn and has earned a professional designation, Certified Financial Planner, earned a Master's degree in Pastoral Ministry from Liberty Theological Seminary, a Doctorate in Biblical Studies from Master's International School of Divinity, and a Ph.D. in Pastoral Ministry from Trinity Theological Seminary. In addition to serving as senior pastor at Hope Family Fellowship, Dr. Klick is a consultant with The Institute for Church Management and also serves on the Board of Directors for The Council for Gospel Legacy Churches. www.jeffklick.com

Rodney Harrison

Dr. Rodney A. Harrison has been in full-time and bi-vocational ministry since 1984. He currently teaches Church Administration at Midwestern Baptist Theological Seminary in Kansas City, where he serves as Vice President for Institutional Effectiveness, Dean of Online Education, and Director of Doctoral Studies. Dr. Harrison holds the D.Min. in Mission Administration and MACE from Golden Gate Seminary and has done post-doctoral studies at Oxford University and post-graduate studies at Southwestern Baptist Theological Seminary. Harrison and his wife, Julie, have three grown children, Joshua, Cassandra, and Gabrielle. In addition to his academic role, he is a frequent conference speaker on church revitalization, conflict mitigation, and issues in church health.

Thank you for reading our thoughts. We trust that God will use this tool to further the work of His Kingdom.

Books and Videos by the Authors

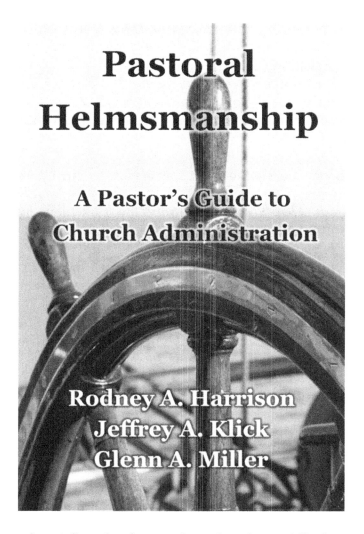

Pastoral Helmsmanship

A Pastor's Guide to Church Administration

Rodney A. Harrison
Jeffrey A. Klick
Glenn A. Miller

The authors' first book together that is rapidly becoming required reading for every pastor and seminary student. Pastors typically will spend 40-60% of their time in administration, yet rarely will they be trained for this expenditure. This book is both a handbook and textbook to help close the gap between training and reality.

Rodney's Books

Seven Steps for Planting New Churches - One of the first books on church planting written from the perspective of the sponsoring church. *Seven Steps* is a practical guide for pastors and church leaders committed to church multiplication.

Spin-Off Churches: How One Church Successfully Plants Another - This comprehensive resource for sponsoring new congregations, and is available in print and e-book formats.

Jeff's Books (available at Amazon.com in print, audio, or Kindle)

Courage to Flee, Second Edition - How to achieve and keep moral freedom.

Gospel Legacy: A Church and Family Model - God's plan for the family explained from a Biblical perspective.

The Master's Handiwork - God is not finished with any of us yet and He never fails, so don't give up or in.

Reaching the Next Generation for Christ: The Biblical Role of the Family and Church - Detailed research on faith impartation to the next generation.

The Discipling Church: Our Great Commission - An in-depth study and training guide on the Great Commission.

A Glimpse Behind the Calling: The Life of a Pastor - Written to help both pastors and those who love them.

Glenn Videos

3 Hour HD - Workshop DVDs available at www.mmsmidwest.com/institute-for-church-management

Fireproof Your Ministry! - Installing affordable internal controls to prevent fraud and increase credibility. A perfect complement to this book.

Church Administrator/Treasurer 101: Understanding the basics of effective church administration - Required for everyone dealing with church administration.

Made in the USA
Coppell, TX
12 October 2021